M000199140

THIS IS YOUR **PASSBOOK**® FOR ...

CLERICAL AIDE

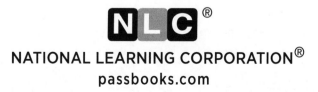

NATIONAL LEARNING CORPORATION®
passbooks.com

PASSBOOK® SERIES

THE *PASSBOOK® SERIES* has been created to prepare applicants and candidates for the ultimate academic battlefield – the examination room.

At some time in our lives, each and every one of us may be required to take an examination – for validation, matriculation, admission, qualification, registration, certification, or licensure.

Based on the assumption that every applicant or candidate has met the basic formal educational standards, has taken the required number of courses, and read the necessary texts, the *PASSBOOK® SERIES* furnishes the one special preparation which may assure passing with confidence, instead of failing with insecurity. Examination questions – together with answers – are furnished as the basic vehicle for study so that the mysteries of the examination and its compounding difficulties may be eliminated or diminished by a sure method.

This book is meant to help you pass your examination provided that you qualify and are serious in your objective.

The entire field is reviewed through the huge store of content information which is succinctly presented through a provocative and challenging approach – the question-and-answer method.

A climate of success is established by furnishing the correct answers at the end of each test.

You soon learn to recognize types of questions, forms of questions, and patterns of questioning. You may even begin to anticipate expected outcomes.

You perceive that many questions are repeated or adapted so that you can gain acute insights, which may enable you to score many sure points.

You learn how to confront new questions, or types of questions, and to attack them confidently and work out the correct answers.

You note objectives and emphases, and recognize pitfalls and dangers, so that you may make positive educational adjustments.

Moreover, you are kept fully informed in relation to new concepts, methods, practices, and directions in the field.

You discover that you arre actually taking the examination all the time: you are preparing for the examination by "taking" an examination, not by reading extraneous and/or supererogatory textbooks.

In short, this PASSBOOK®, used directedly, should be an important factor in helping you to pass your test.

CLERICAL AIDE

DUTIES

Clerical Aides, under direct supervision, perform routine clerical work of minimal difficulty and responsibility with very limited latitude for independent judgment. All Clerical Aides perform related work.

THE SCOPE OF THE EXAMINATION

The multiple-choice test is designed to assess the extent to which candidates have certain abilities determined to be important to the performance of the tasks of a Clerical Aide. Task areas to be tested are as follows: clerical duties; records management; word processing and data entry; and communication responsibilities. The test may include questions requiring the use of any of the following abilities: matching, deductive reasoning, information ordering, number facility and inductive reasoning.

HOW TO TAKE A TEST

I. YOU MUST PASS AN EXAMINATION

A. *WHAT EVERY CANDIDATE SHOULD KNOW*

Examination applicants often ask us for help in preparing for the written test. What can I study in advance? What kinds of questions will be asked? How will the test be given? How will the papers be graded?

As an applicant for a civil service examination, you may be wondering about some of these things. Our purpose here is to suggest effective methods of advance study and to describe civil service examinations.

Your chances for success on this examination can be increased if you know how to prepare. Those "pre-examination jitters" can be reduced if you know what to expect. You can even experience an adventure in good citizenship if you know why civil service exams are given.

B. *WHY ARE CIVIL SERVICE EXAMINATIONS GIVEN?*

Civil service examinations are important to you in two ways. As a citizen, you want public jobs filled by employees who know how to do their work. As a job seeker, you want a fair chance to compete for that job on an equal footing with other candidates. The best-known means of accomplishing this two-fold goal is the competitive examination.

Exams are widely publicized throughout the nation. They may be administered for jobs in federal, state, city, municipal, town or village governments or agencies.

Any citizen may apply, with some limitations, such as the age or residence of applicants. Your experience and education may be reviewed to see whether you meet the requirements for the particular examination. When these requirements exist, they are reasonable and applied consistently to all applicants. Thus, a competitive examination may cause you some uneasiness now, but it is your privilege and safeguard.

C. *HOW ARE CIVIL SERVICE EXAMS DEVELOPED?*

Examinations are carefully written by trained technicians who are specialists in the field known as "psychological measurement," in consultation with recognized authorities in the field of work that the test will cover. These experts recommend the subject matter areas or skills to be tested; only those knowledges or skills important to your success on the job are included. The most reliable books and source materials available are used as references. Together, the experts and technicians judge the difficulty level of the questions.

Test technicians know how to phrase questions so that the problem is clearly stated. Their ethics do not permit "trick" or "catch" questions. Questions may have been tried out on sample groups, or subjected to statistical analysis, to determine their usefulness.

Written tests are often used in combination with performance tests, ratings of training and experience, and oral interviews. All of these measures combine to form the best-known means of finding the right person for the right job.

II. HOW TO PASS THE WRITTEN TEST

A. NATURE OF THE EXAMINATION

To prepare intelligently for civil service examinations, you should know how they differ from school examinations you have taken. In school you were assigned certain definite pages to read or subjects to cover. The examination questions were quite detailed and usually emphasized memory. Civil service exams, on the other hand, try to discover your present ability to perform the duties of a position, plus your potentiality to learn these duties. In other words, a civil service exam attempts to predict how successful you will be. Questions cover such a broad area that they cannot be as minute and detailed as school exam questions.

In the public service similar kinds of work, or positions, are grouped together in one "class." This process is known as *position-classification*. All the positions in a class are paid according to the salary range for that class. One class title covers all of these positions, and they are all tested by the same examination.

B. FOUR BASIC STEPS

1) Study the announcement

How, then, can you know what subjects to study? Our best answer is: "Learn as much as possible about the class of positions for which you've applied." The exam will test the knowledge, skills and abilities needed to do the work.

Your most valuable source of information about the position you want is the official exam announcement. This announcement lists the training and experience qualifications. Check these standards and apply only if you come reasonably close to meeting them.

The brief description of the position in the examination announcement offers some clues to the subjects which will be tested. Think about the job itself. Review the duties in your mind. Can you perform them, or are there some in which you are rusty? Fill in the blank spots in your preparation.

Many jurisdictions preview the written test in the exam announcement by including a section called "Knowledge and Abilities Required," "Scope of the Examination," or some similar heading. Here you will find out specifically what fields will be tested.

2) Review your own background

Once you learn in general what the position is all about, and what you need to know to do the work, ask yourself which subjects you already know fairly well and which need improvement. You may wonder whether to concentrate on improving your strong areas or on building some background in your fields of weakness. When the announcement has specified "some knowledge" or "considerable knowledge," or has used adjectives like "beginning principles of…" or "advanced … methods," you can get a clue as to the number and difficulty of questions to be asked in any given field. More questions, and hence broader coverage, would be included for those subjects which are more important in the work. Now weigh your strengths and weaknesses against the job requirements and prepare accordingly.

3) Determine the level of the position

Another way to tell how intensively you should prepare is to understand the level of the job for which you are applying. Is it the entering level? In other words, is this the position in which beginners in a field of work are hired? Or is it an intermediate or advanced level? Sometimes this is indicated by such words as "Junior" or "Senior" in the class title. Other jurisdictions use Roman numerals to designate the level – Clerk I, Clerk II, for example. The word "Supervisor" sometimes appears in the title. If the level is not indicated by the title, check the description of duties. Will you be working under very close supervision, or will you have responsibility for independent decisions in this work?

4) Choose appropriate study materials

Now that you know the subjects to be examined and the relative amount of each subject to be covered, you can choose suitable study materials. For beginning level jobs, or even advanced ones, if you have a pronounced weakness in some aspect of your training, read a modern, standard textbook in that field. Be sure it is up to date and has general coverage. Such books are normally available at your library, and the librarian will be glad to help you locate one. For entry-level positions, questions of appropriate difficulty are chosen – neither highly advanced questions, nor those too simple. Such questions require careful thought but not advanced training.

If the position for which you are applying is technical or advanced, you will read more advanced, specialized material. If you are already familiar with the basic principles of your field, elementary textbooks would waste your time. Concentrate on advanced textbooks and technical periodicals. Think through the concepts and review difficult problems in your field.

These are all general sources. You can get more ideas on your own initiative, following these leads. For example, training manuals and publications of the government agency which employs workers in your field can be useful, particularly for technical and professional positions. A letter or visit to the government department involved may result in more specific study suggestions, and certainly will provide you with a more definite idea of the exact nature of the position you are seeking.

III. KINDS OF TESTS

Tests are used for purposes other than measuring knowledge and ability to perform specified duties. For some positions, it is equally important to test ability to make adjustments to new situations or to profit from training. In others, basic mental abilities not dependent on information are essential. Questions which test these things may not appear as pertinent to the duties of the position as those which test for knowledge and information. Yet they are often highly important parts of a fair examination. For very general questions, it is almost impossible to help you direct your study efforts. What we can do is to point out some of the more common of these general abilities needed in public service positions and describe some typical questions.

1) General information

Broad, general information has been found useful for predicting job success in some kinds of work. This is tested in a variety of ways, from vocabulary lists to questions about current events. Basic background in some field of work, such as sociology or economics, may be sampled in a group of questions. Often these are principles which have become familiar to most persons through exposure rather than through formal training. It is difficult to advise you how to study for these questions; being alert to the world around you is our best suggestion.

2) Verbal ability

An example of an ability needed in many positions is verbal or language ability. Verbal ability is, in brief, the ability to use and understand words. Vocabulary and grammar tests are typical measures of this ability. Reading comprehension or paragraph interpretation questions are common in many kinds of civil service tests. You are given a paragraph of written material and asked to find its central meaning.

3) Numerical ability

Number skills can be tested by the familiar arithmetic problem, by checking paired lists of numbers to see which are alike and which are different, or by interpreting charts and graphs. In the latter test, a graph may be printed in the test booklet which you are asked to use as the basis for answering questions.

4) Observation

A popular test for law-enforcement positions is the observation test. A picture is shown to you for several minutes, then taken away. Questions about the picture test your ability to observe both details and larger elements.

5) Following directions

In many positions in the public service, the employee must be able to carry out written instructions dependably and accurately. You may be given a chart with several columns, each column listing a variety of information. The questions require you to carry out directions involving the information given in the chart.

6) Skills and aptitudes

Performance tests effectively measure some manual skills and aptitudes. When the skill is one in which you are trained, such as typing or shorthand, you can practice. These tests are often very much like those given in business school or high school courses. For many of the other skills and aptitudes, however, no short-time preparation can be made. Skills and abilities natural to you or that you have developed throughout your lifetime are being tested.

Many of the general questions just described provide all the data needed to answer the questions and ask you to use your reasoning ability to find the answers. Your best preparation for these tests, as well as for tests of facts and ideas, is to be at your physical and mental best. You, no doubt, have your own methods of getting into an exam-taking mood and keeping "in shape." The next section lists some ideas on this subject.

IV. KINDS OF QUESTIONS

Only rarely is the "essay" question, which you answer in narrative form, used in civil service tests. Civil service tests are usually of the short-answer type. Full instructions for answering these questions will be given to you at the examination. But in case this is your first experience with short-answer questions and separate answer sheets, here is what you need to know:

1) Multiple-choice Questions

Most popular of the short-answer questions is the "multiple choice" or "best answer" question. It can be used, for example, to test for factual knowledge, ability to solve problems or judgment in meeting situations found at work.

A multiple-choice question is normally one of three types—

- It can begin with an incomplete statement followed by several possible endings. You are to find the one ending which *best* completes the statement, although some of the others may not be entirely wrong.
- It can also be a complete statement in the form of a question which is answered by choosing one of the statements listed.
- It can be in the form of a problem – again you select the best answer.

Here is an example of a multiple-choice question with a discussion which should give you some clues as to the method for choosing the right answer:

When an employee has a complaint about his assignment, the action which will *best* help him overcome his difficulty is to
- A. discuss his difficulty with his coworkers
- B. take the problem to the head of the organization
- C. take the problem to the person who gave him the assignment
- D. say nothing to anyone about his complaint

In answering this question, you should study each of the choices to find which is best. Consider choice "A" – Certainly an employee may discuss his complaint with fellow employees, but no change or improvement can result, and the complaint remains unresolved. Choice "B" is a poor choice since the head of the organization probably does not know what assignment you have been given, and taking your problem to him is known as "going over the head" of the supervisor. The supervisor, or person who made the assignment, is the person who can clarify it or correct any injustice. Choice "C" is, therefore, correct. To say nothing, as in choice "D," is unwise. Supervisors have and interest in knowing the problems employees are facing, and the employee is seeking a solution to his problem.

2) True/False Questions

The "true/false" or "right/wrong" form of question is sometimes used. Here a complete statement is given. Your job is to decide whether the statement is right or wrong.

SAMPLE: A roaming cell-phone call to a nearby city costs less than a non-roaming call to a distant city.

This statement is wrong, or false, since roaming calls are more expensive.

This is not a complete list of all possible question forms, although most of the others are variations of these common types. You will always get complete directions for answering questions. Be sure you understand *how* to mark your answers – ask questions until you do.

V. RECORDING YOUR ANSWERS

Computer terminals are used more and more today for many different kinds of exams.

For an examination with very few applicants, you may be told to record your answers in the test booklet itself. Separate answer sheets are much more common. If this separate answer sheet is to be scored by machine – and this is often the case – it is highly important that you mark your answers correctly in order to get credit.

An electronic scoring machine is often used in civil service offices because of the speed with which papers can be scored. Machine-scored answer sheets must be marked with a pencil, which will be given to you. This pencil has a high graphite content which responds to the electronic scoring machine. As a matter of fact, stray dots may register as answers, so do not let your pencil rest on the answer sheet while you are pondering the correct answer. Also, if your pencil lead breaks or is otherwise defective, ask for another.

Since the answer sheet will be dropped in a slot in the scoring machine, be careful not to bend the corners or get the paper crumpled.

The answer sheet normally has five vertical columns of numbers, with 30 numbers to a column. These numbers correspond to the question numbers in your test booklet. After each number, going across the page are four or five pairs of dotted lines. These short dotted lines have small letters or numbers above them. The first two pairs may also have a "T" or "F" above the letters. This indicates that the first two pairs only are to be used if the questions are of the true-false type. If the questions are multiple choice, disregard the "T" and "F" and pay attention only to the small letters or numbers.

Answer your questions in the manner of the sample that follows:

32. The largest city in the United States is
    A. Washington, D.C.
    B. New York City
    C. Chicago
    D. Detroit
    E. San Francisco

1) Choose the answer you think is best. (New York City is the largest, so "B" is correct.)
2) Find the row of dotted lines numbered the same as the question you are answering. (Find row number 32)
3) Find the pair of dotted lines corresponding to the answer. (Find the pair of lines under the mark "B.")
4) Make a solid black mark between the dotted lines.

VI. BEFORE THE TEST

Common sense will help you find procedures to follow to get ready for an examination. Too many of us, however, overlook these sensible measures. Indeed, nervousness and fatigue have been found to be the most serious reasons why applicants fail to do their best on civil service tests. Here is a list of reminders:

- Begin your preparation early – Don't wait until the last minute to go scurrying around for books and materials or to find out what the position is all about.
- Prepare continuously – An hour a night for a week is better than an all-night cram session. This has been definitely established. What is more, a night a week for a month will return better dividends than crowding your study into a shorter period of time.
- Locate the place of the exam – You have been sent a notice telling you when and where to report for the examination. If the location is in a different town or otherwise unfamiliar to you, it would be well to inquire the best route and learn something about the building.
- Relax the night before the test – Allow your mind to rest. Do not study at all that night. Plan some mild recreation or diversion; then go to bed early and get a good night's sleep.
- Get up early enough to make a leisurely trip to the place for the test – This way unforeseen events, traffic snarls, unfamiliar buildings, etc. will not upset you.
- Dress comfortably – A written test is not a fashion show. You will be known by number and not by name, so wear something comfortable.
- Leave excess paraphernalia at home – Shopping bags and odd bundles will get in your way. You need bring only the items mentioned in the official notice you received; usually everything you need is provided. Do not bring reference books to the exam. They will only confuse those last minutes and be taken away from you when in the test room.
- Arrive somewhat ahead of time – If because of transportation schedules you must get there very early, bring a newspaper or magazine to take your mind off yourself while waiting.
- Locate the examination room – When you have found the proper room, you will be directed to the seat or part of the room where you will sit. Sometimes you are given a sheet of instructions to read while you are waiting. Do not fill out any forms until you are told to do so; just read them and be prepared.
- Relax and prepare to listen to the instructions
- If you have any physical problem that may keep you from doing your best, be sure to tell the test administrator. If you are sick or in poor health, you really cannot do your best on the exam. You can come back and take the test some other time.

VII. AT THE TEST

The day of the test is here and you have the test booklet in your hand. The temptation to get going is very strong. Caution! There is more to success than knowing the right answers. You must know how to identify your papers and understand variations in the type of short-answer question used in this particular examination. Follow these suggestions for maximum results from your efforts:

1) Cooperate with the monitor

The test administrator has a duty to create a situation in which you can be as much at ease as possible. He will give instructions, tell you when to begin, check to see that you are marking your answer sheet correctly, and so on. He is not there to guard you, although he will see that your competitors do not take unfair advantage. He wants to help you do your best.

2) Listen to all instructions

Don't jump the gun! Wait until you understand all directions. In most civil service tests you get more time than you need to answer the questions. So don't be in a hurry. Read each word of instructions until you clearly understand the meaning. Study the examples, listen to all announcements and follow directions. Ask questions if you do not understand what to do.

3) Identify your papers

Civil service exams are usually identified by number only. You will be assigned a number; you must not put your name on your test papers. Be sure to copy your number correctly. Since more than one exam may be given, copy your exact examination title.

4) Plan your time

Unless you are told that a test is a "speed" or "rate of work" test, speed itself is usually not important. Time enough to answer all the questions will be provided, but this does not mean that you have all day. An overall time limit has been set. Divide the total time (in minutes) by the number of questions to determine the approximate time you have for each question.

5) Do not linger over difficult questions

If you come across a difficult question, mark it with a paper clip (useful to have along) and come back to it when you have been through the booklet. One caution if you do this – be sure to skip a number on your answer sheet as well. Check often to be sure that you have not lost your place and that you are marking in the row numbered the same as the question you are answering.

6) Read the questions

Be sure you know what the question asks! Many capable people are unsuccessful because they failed to *read* the questions correctly.

7) Answer all questions

Unless you have been instructed that a penalty will be deducted for incorrect answers, it is better to guess than to omit a question.

8) Speed tests

It is often better NOT to guess on speed tests. It has been found that on timed tests people are tempted to spend the last few seconds before time is called in marking answers at random – without even reading them – in the hope of picking up a few extra points. To discourage this practice, the instructions may warn you that your score will be "corrected" for guessing. That is, a penalty will be applied. The incorrect answers will be deducted from the correct ones, or some other penalty formula will be used.

9) Review your answers

If you finish before time is called, go back to the questions you guessed or omitted to give them further thought. Review other answers if you have time.

10) Return your test materials

If you are ready to leave before others have finished or time is called, take ALL your materials to the monitor and leave quietly. Never take any test material with you. The monitor can discover whose papers are not complete, and taking a test booklet may be grounds for disqualification.

VIII. EXAMINATION TECHNIQUES

1) Read the general instructions carefully. These are usually printed on the first page of the exam booklet. As a rule, these instructions refer to the timing of the examination; the fact that you should not start work until the signal and must stop work at a signal, etc. If there are any *special* instructions, such as a choice of questions to be answered, make sure that you note this instruction carefully.

2) When you are ready to start work on the examination, that is as soon as the signal has been given, read the instructions to each question booklet, underline any key words or phrases, such as *least, best, outline, describe* and the like. In this way you will tend to answer as requested rather than discover on reviewing your paper that you *listed without describing*, that you selected the *worst* choice rather than the *best* choice, etc.

3) If the examination is of the objective or multiple-choice type – that is, each question will also give a series of possible answers: A, B, C or D, and you are called upon to select the best answer and write the letter next to that answer on your answer paper – it is advisable to start answering each question in turn. There may be anywhere from 50 to 100 such questions in the three or four hours allotted and you can see how much time would be taken if you read through all the questions before beginning to answer any. Furthermore, if you come across a question or group of questions which you know would be difficult to answer, it would undoubtedly affect your handling of all the other questions.

4) If the examination is of the essay type and contains but a few questions, it is a moot point as to whether you should read all the questions before starting to answer any one. Of course, if you are given a choice – say five out of seven and the like – then it is essential to read all the questions so you can eliminate the two that are most difficult. If, however, you are asked to answer all the questions, there may be danger in trying to answer the easiest one first because you may find that you will spend too much time on it. The best technique is to answer the first question, then proceed to the second, etc.

5) Time your answers. Before the exam begins, write down the time it started, then add the time allowed for the examination and write down the time it must be completed, then divide the time available somewhat as follows:

- If 3-1/2 hours are allowed, that would be 210 minutes. If you have 80 objective-type questions, that would be an average of 2-1/2 minutes per question. Allow yourself no more than 2 minutes per question, or a total of 160 minutes, which will permit about 50 minutes to review.
- If for the time allotment of 210 minutes there are 7 essay questions to answer, that would average about 30 minutes a question. Give yourself only 25 minutes per question so that you have about 35 minutes to review.

6) The most important instruction is to *read each question* and make sure you know what is wanted. The second most important instruction is to *time yourself properly* so that you answer every question. The third most important instruction is to *answer every question.* Guess if you have to but include something for each question. Remember that you will receive no credit for a blank and will probably receive some credit if you write something in answer to an essay question. If you guess a letter – say "B" for a multiple-choice question – you may have guessed right. If you leave a blank as an answer to a multiple-choice question, the examiners may respect your feelings but it will not add a point to your score. Some exams may penalize you for wrong answers, so in such cases *only*, you may not want to guess unless you have some basis for your answer.

7) Suggestions
   a. Objective-type questions
      1. Examine the question booklet for proper sequence of pages and questions
      2. Read all instructions carefully
      3. Skip any question which seems too difficult; return to it after all other questions have been answered
      4. Apportion your time properly; do not spend too much time on any single question or group of questions
      5. Note and underline key words – *all, most, fewest, least, best, worst, same, opposite,* etc.
      6. Pay particular attention to negatives
      7. Note unusual option, e.g., unduly long, short, complex, different or similar in content to the body of the question
      8. Observe the use of "hedging" words – *probably, may, most likely,* etc.
      9. Make sure that your answer is put next to the same number as the question
      10. Do not second-guess unless you have good reason to believe the second answer is definitely more correct
      11. Cross out original answer if you decide another answer is more accurate; do not erase until you are ready to hand your paper in
      12. Answer all questions; guess unless instructed otherwise
      13. Leave time for review

   b. Essay questions
      1. Read each question carefully
      2. Determine exactly what is wanted. Underline key words or phrases.
      3. Decide on outline or paragraph answer

4. Include many different points and elements unless asked to develop any one or two points or elements
5. Show impartiality by giving pros and cons unless directed to select one side only
6. Make and write down any assumptions you find necessary to answer the questions
7. Watch your English, grammar, punctuation and choice of words
8. Time your answers; don't crowd material

8) Answering the essay question

Most essay questions can be answered by framing the specific response around several key words or ideas. Here are a few such key words or ideas:

M's: manpower, materials, methods, money, management
P's: purpose, program, policy, plan, procedure, practice, problems, pitfalls, personnel, public relations
  a. Six basic steps in handling problems:
     1. Preliminary plan and background development
     2. Collect information, data and facts
     3. Analyze and interpret information, data and facts
     4. Analyze and develop solutions as well as make recommendations
     5. Prepare report and sell recommendations
     6. Install recommendations and follow up effectiveness

  b. Pitfalls to avoid
     1. *Taking things for granted* – A statement of the situation does not necessarily imply that each of the elements is necessarily true; for example, a complaint may be invalid and biased so that all that can be taken for granted is that a complaint has been registered
     2. *Considering only one side of a situation* – Wherever possible, indicate several alternatives and then point out the reasons you selected the best one
     3. *Failing to indicate follow up* – Whenever your answer indicates action on your part, make certain that you will take proper follow-up action to see how successful your recommendations, procedures or actions turn out to be
     4. *Taking too long in answering any single question* – Remember to time your answers properly

IX. AFTER THE TEST

Scoring procedures differ in detail among civil service jurisdictions although the general principles are the same. Whether the papers are hand-scored or graded by machine we have described, they are nearly always graded by number. That is, the person who marks the paper knows only the number – never the name – of the applicant. Not until all the papers have been graded will they be matched with names. If other tests, such as training and experience or oral interview ratings have been given, scores will be combined. Different parts of the examination usually have different weights. For example, the written test might count 60 percent of the final grade, and a rating of training and experience 40 percent. In many jurisdictions, veterans will have a certain number of points added to their grades.

After the final grade has been determined, the names are placed in grade order and an eligible list is established. There are various methods for resolving ties between those who get the same final grade – probably the most common is to place first the name of the person whose application was received first. Job offers are made from the eligible list in the order the names appear on it. You will be notified of your grade and your rank as soon as all these computations have been made. This will be done as rapidly as possible.

People who are found to meet the requirements in the announcement are called "eligibles." Their names are put on a list of eligible candidates. An eligible's chances of getting a job depend on how high he stands on this list and how fast agencies are filling jobs from the list.

When a job is to be filled from a list of eligibles, the agency asks for the names of people on the list of eligibles for that job. When the civil service commission receives this request, it sends to the agency the names of the three people highest on this list. Or, if the job to be filled has specialized requirements, the office sends the agency the names of the top three persons who meet these requirements from the general list.

The appointing officer makes a choice from among the three people whose names were sent to him. If the selected person accepts the appointment, the names of the others are put back on the list to be considered for future openings.

That is the rule in hiring from all kinds of eligible lists, whether they are for typist, carpenter, chemist, or something else. For every vacancy, the appointing officer has his choice of any one of the top three eligibles on the list. This explains why the person whose name is on top of the list sometimes does not get an appointment when some of the persons lower on the list do. If the appointing officer chooses the second or third eligible, the No. 1 eligible does not get a job at once, but stays on the list until he is appointed or the list is terminated.

X. HOW TO PASS THE INTERVIEW TEST

The examination for which you applied requires an oral interview test. You have already taken the written test and you are now being called for the interview test – the final part of the formal examination.

You may think that it is not possible to prepare for an interview test and that there are no procedures to follow during an interview. Our purpose is to point out some things you can do in advance that will help you and some good rules to follow and pitfalls to avoid while you are being interviewed.

What is an interview supposed to test?

The written examination is designed to test the technical knowledge and competence of the candidate; the oral is designed to evaluate intangible qualities, not readily measured otherwise, and to establish a list showing the relative fitness of each candidate – as measured against his competitors – for the position sought. Scoring is not on the basis of "right" and "wrong," but on a sliding scale of values ranging from "not passable" to "outstanding." As a matter of fact, it is possible to achieve a relatively low score without a single "incorrect" answer because of evident weakness in the qualities being measured.

Occasionally, an examination may consist entirely of an oral test – either an individual or a group oral. In such cases, information is sought concerning the technical knowledges and abilities of the candidate, since there has been no written examination for this purpose. More commonly, however, an oral test is used to supplement a written examination.

Who conducts interviews?

The composition of oral boards varies among different jurisdictions. In nearly all, a representative of the personnel department serves as chairman. One of the members of the board may be a representative of the department in which the candidate would work. In some cases, "outside experts" are used, and, frequently, a businessman or some other representative of the general public is asked to serve. Labor and management or other special groups may be represented. The aim is to secure the services of experts in the appropriate field.

However the board is composed, it is a good idea (and not at all improper or unethical) to ascertain in advance of the interview who the members are and what groups they represent. When you are introduced to them, you will have some idea of their backgrounds and interests, and at least you will not stutter and stammer over their names.

What should be done before the interview?

While knowledge about the board members is useful and takes some of the surprise element out of the interview, there is other preparation which is more substantive. It *is* possible to prepare for an oral interview – in several ways:

1) Keep a copy of your application and review it carefully before the interview

This may be the only document before the oral board, and the starting point of the interview. Know what education and experience you have listed there, and the sequence and dates of all of it. Sometimes the board will ask you to review the highlights of your experience for them; you should not have to hem and haw doing it.

2) Study the class specification and the examination announcement

Usually, the oral board has one or both of these to guide them. The qualities, characteristics or knowledges required by the position sought are stated in these documents. They offer valuable clues as to the nature of the oral interview. For example, if the job involves supervisory responsibilities, the announcement will usually indicate that knowledge of modern supervisory methods and the qualifications of the candidate as a supervisor will be tested. If so, you can expect such questions, frequently in the form of a hypothetical situation which you are expected to solve. NEVER go into an oral without knowledge of the duties and responsibilities of the job you seek.

3) Think through each qualification required

Try to visualize the kind of questions you would ask if you were a board member. How well could you answer them? Try especially to appraise your own knowledge and background in each area, *measured against the job sought*, and identify any areas in which you are weak. Be critical and realistic – do not flatter yourself.

4) Do some general reading in areas in which you feel you may be weak

For example, if the job involves supervision and your past experience has NOT, some general reading in supervisory methods and practices, particularly in the field of human relations, might be useful. Do NOT study agency procedures or detailed manuals. The oral board will be testing your understanding and capacity, not your memory.

5) Get a good night's sleep and watch your general health and mental attitude

You will want a clear head at the interview. Take care of a cold or any other minor ailment, and of course, no hangovers.

What should be done on the day of the interview?

Now comes the day of the interview itself. Give yourself plenty of time to get there. Plan to arrive somewhat ahead of the scheduled time, particularly if your appointment is in the fore part of the day. If a previous candidate fails to appear, the board might be ready for you a bit early. By early afternoon an oral board is almost invariably behind schedule if there are many candidates, and you may have to wait. Take along a book or magazine to read, or your application to review, but leave any extraneous material in the waiting room when you go in for your interview. In any event, relax and compose yourself.

The matter of dress is important. The board is forming impressions about you – from your experience, your manners, your attitude, and your appearance. Give your personal appearance careful attention. Dress your best, but not your flashiest. Choose conservative, appropriate clothing, and be sure it is immaculate. This is a business interview, and your appearance should indicate that you regard it as such. Besides, being well groomed and properly dressed will help boost your confidence.

Sooner or later, someone will call your name and escort you into the interview room. *This is it.* From here on you are on your own. It is too late for any more preparation. But remember, you asked for this opportunity to prove your fitness, and you are here because your request was granted.

What happens when you go in?

The usual sequence of events will be as follows: The clerk (who is often the board stenographer) will introduce you to the chairman of the oral board, who will introduce you to the other members of the board. Acknowledge the introductions before you sit down. Do not be surprised if you find a microphone facing you or a stenotypist sitting by. Oral interviews are usually recorded in the event of an appeal or other review.

Usually the chairman of the board will open the interview by reviewing the highlights of your education and work experience from your application – primarily for the benefit of the other members of the board, as well as to get the material into the record. Do not interrupt or comment unless there is an error or significant misinterpretation; if that is the case, do not hesitate. But do not quibble about insignificant matters. Also, he will usually ask you some question about your education, experience or your present job – partly to get you to start talking and to establish the interviewing "rapport." He may start the actual questioning, or turn it over to one of the other members. Frequently, each member undertakes the questioning on a particular area, one in which he is perhaps most competent, so you can expect each member to participate in the examination. Because time is limited, you may also expect some rather abrupt switches in the direction the questioning takes, so do not be upset by it. Normally, a board member will not pursue a single line of questioning unless he discovers a particular strength or weakness.

After each member has participated, the chairman will usually ask whether any member has any further questions, then will ask you if you have anything you wish to add. Unless you are expecting this question, it may floor you. Worse, it may start you off on an extended, extemporaneous speech. The board is not usually seeking more information. The question is principally to offer you a last opportunity to present further qualifications or to indicate that you have nothing to add. So, if you feel that a significant qualification or characteristic has been overlooked, it is proper to point it out in a sentence or so. Do not compliment the board on the thoroughness of their examination – they have been sketchy, and you know it. If you wish, merely say, "No thank you, I have nothing further to add." This is a point where you can "talk yourself out" of a good impression or fail to present an important bit of information. Remember, *you close the interview yourself.*

The chairman will then say, "That is all, Mr. _____, thank you." Do not be startled; the interview is over, and quicker than you think. Thank him, gather your belongings and take your leave. Save your sigh of relief for the other side of the door.

How to put your best foot forward

Throughout this entire process, you may feel that the board individually and collectively is trying to pierce your defenses, seek out your hidden weaknesses and embarrass and confuse you. Actually, this is not true. They are obliged to make an appraisal of your qualifications for the job you are seeking, and they want to see you in your best light. Remember, they must interview all candidates and a non-cooperative candidate may become a failure in spite of their best efforts to bring out his qualifications. Here are 15 suggestions that will help you:

1) Be natural – Keep your attitude confident, not cocky

If you are not confident that you can do the job, do not expect the board to be. Do not apologize for your weaknesses, try to bring out your strong points. The board is interested in a positive, not negative, presentation. Cockiness will antagonize any board member and make him wonder if you are covering up a weakness by a false show of strength.

2) Get comfortable, but don't lounge or sprawl

Sit erectly but not stiffly. A careless posture may lead the board to conclude that you are careless in other things, or at least that you are not impressed by the importance of the occasion. Either conclusion is natural, even if incorrect. Do not fuss with your clothing, a pencil or an ashtray. Your hands may occasionally be useful to emphasize a point; do not let them become a point of distraction.

3) Do not wisecrack or make small talk

This is a serious situation, and your attitude should show that you consider it as such. Further, the time of the board is limited – they do not want to waste it, and neither should you.

4) Do not exaggerate your experience or abilities

In the first place, from information in the application or other interviews and sources, the board may know more about you than you think. Secondly, you probably will not get away with it. An experienced board is rather adept at spotting such a situation, so do not take the chance.

5) If you know a board member, do not make a point of it, yet do not hide it

Certainly you are not fooling him, and probably not the other members of the board. Do not try to take advantage of your acquaintanceship – it will probably do you little good.

6) Do not dominate the interview

Let the board do that. They will give you the clues – do not assume that you have to do all the talking. Realize that the board has a number of questions to ask you, and do not try to take up all the interview time by showing off your extensive knowledge of the answer to the first one.

7) Be attentive

You only have 20 minutes or so, and you should keep your attention at its sharpest throughout. When a member is addressing a problem or question to you, give him your undivided attention. Address your reply principally to him, but do not exclude the other board members.

8) Do not interrupt

A board member may be stating a problem for you to analyze. He will ask you a question when the time comes. Let him state the problem, and wait for the question.

9) Make sure you understand the question

Do not try to answer until you are sure what the question is. If it is not clear, restate it in your own words or ask the board member to clarify it for you. However, do not haggle about minor elements.

10) Reply promptly but not hastily

A common entry on oral board rating sheets is "candidate responded readily," or "candidate hesitated in replies." Respond as promptly and quickly as you can, but do not jump to a hasty, ill-considered answer.

11) Do not be peremptory in your answers

A brief answer is proper – but do not fire your answer back. That is a losing game from your point of view. The board member can probably ask questions much faster than you can answer them.

12) Do not try to create the answer you think the board member wants

He is interested in what kind of mind you have and how it works – not in playing games. Furthermore, he can usually spot this practice and will actually grade you down on it.

13) Do not switch sides in your reply merely to agree with a board member

Frequently, a member will take a contrary position merely to draw you out and to see if you are willing and able to defend your point of view. Do not start a debate, yet do not surrender a good position. If a position is worth taking, it is worth defending.

14) Do not be afraid to admit an error in judgment if you are shown to be wrong

The board knows that you are forced to reply without any opportunity for careful consideration. Your answer may be demonstrably wrong. If so, admit it and get on with the interview.

15) Do not dwell at length on your present job

The opening question may relate to your present assignment. Answer the question but do not go into an extended discussion. You are being examined for a *new* job, not your present one. As a matter of fact, try to phrase ALL your answers in terms of the job for which you are being examined.

Basis of Rating

Probably you will forget most of these "do's" and "don'ts" when you walk into the oral interview room. Even remembering them all will not ensure you a passing grade. Perhaps you did not have the qualifications in the first place. But remembering them will help you to put your best foot forward, without treading on the toes of the board members.

Rumor and popular opinion to the contrary notwithstanding, an oral board wants you to make the best appearance possible. They know you are under pressure – but they also want to see how you respond to it as a guide to what your reaction would be under the pressures of the job you seek. They will be influenced by the degree of poise you display, the personal traits you show and the manner in which you respond.

ABOUT THIS BOOK

This book contains tests divided into Examination Sections. Go through each test, answering every question in the margin. At the end of each test look at the answer key and check your answers. On the ones you got wrong, look at the right answer choice and learn. Do not fill in the answers first. Do not memorize the questions and answers, but understand the answer and principles involved. On your test, the questions will likely be different from the samples. Questions are changed and new ones added. If you understand these past questions you should have success with any changes that arise. Tests may consist of several types of questions. We have additional books on each subject should more study be advisable or necessary for you. Finally, the more you study, the better prepared you will be. This book is intended to be the last thing you study before you walk into the examination room. Prior study of relevant texts is also recommended. NLC publishes some of these in our Fundamental Series. Knowledge and good sense are important factors in passing your exam. Good luck also helps. So now study this Passbook, absorb the material contained within and take that knowledge into the examination. Then do your best to pass that exam.

———

EXAMINATION SECTION

EXAMINATION SECTION
TEST 1

DIRECTIONS: Each question or incomplete statement is followed by several suggested answers or completions. Select the one that BEST answers the question or completes the statement. *PRINT THE LETTER OF THE CORRECT ANSWER IN THE SPACE AT THE RIGHT.*

1. In considering a new word processing system for a regional office, which of the following would MOST likely be the MOST important consideration in making a decision?

   A. Ease of operation
   B. Friendliness of service technicians
   C. Availability of service technicians
   D. Capacity of the system to meet the unit's word processing needs

   1.____

2. Your supervisor is out of town for several days and has asked you to act as supervisor in his absence. An employee in the unit comes to you and complains that the supervisor has been dividing the workload unfairly.
   Of the following, the MOST appropriate action for you to take is

   A. defend the actions of your supervisor
   B. encourage the employee to file a grievance
   C. listen to the employee attentively
   D. explain to the employee that you have no authority to handle the situation

   2.____

3. A principal stenographer still on probation is instructed to supervise and coordinate the completion of a large word processing project. Her supervisor asks her how long she thinks the project will take. The principal stenographer gives her supervisor an estimate that is two days longer than she actually thinks the project will take to complete. The project is completed two days earlier, and the principal stenographer is congratulated by her supervisor for her efforts.
   In purposely overestimating the time required to complete the project, the principal stenographer showed

   A. *good* judgment because it helped her appear very efficient
   B. *good* judgment because it helps keep unrealistic supervisors from expecting too much
   C. *poor* judgment because plans and schedules of other components of the project may have been based on her false estimate
   D. *poor* judgment because she should have used the extra time to further check and, proofread the work

   3.____

4. Which of the following would MOST likely be the MOST important in providing support to one's supervisor?

   A. Screening annoying phone calls
   B. Reviewing and forwarding articles and publications that may be of interest to your supervisor
   C. Correctly transmitting instructions from the supervisor to appropriate staff members
   D. Reviewing outgoing correspondence for proper grammatical usage and clarity

   4.____

5. While you are on the telephone answering a question about your agency, a visitor comes   5.____
to your desk and starts to ask you a question. There is no emergency or urgency in either
situation, that of the phone call or that of answering the visitor's question.
In this case, you should

    A. excuse yourself to the person on the telephone and tell the visitor that you will be
with him or her as soon as you have finished on the phone
    B. explain to the person on the phone that you have a visitor and must shorten the
conversation
    C. continue to talk with the person on the phone while looking up occasionally at the
visitor to let him or her know that you know he or she is there
    D. continue to talk with the person on the telephone until you are finished and then let
the visitor know that you're sorry to have kept him or her waiting

6. Your supervisor is out of town on vacation for one week, and asks you to act as supervi-   6.____
sor in her absence. The second day she is gone a very important, complex budgetary
form, which must be responded to in ten days, arrives in your unit.
Of the following, it would be BEST if you

    A. filled out the form and submitted it as soon as possible
    B. read the form over, did any time-consuming research that might be needed, and
then gave the uncompleted form to your supervisor as soon as she returned
    C. asked for help from your supervisor's supervisor in completing the form
    D. tried to contact your supervisor for advice

7. Of the following, which would MOST likely be of the highest priority?   7.____
The typing of

    A. a grant proposal due next week
    B. new addresses onto a mailing list for a future mailing
    C. a payroll form for a new employee that needs to be submitted immediately
    D. a memorandum from the Commissioner to all employees regarding new proce-
dures

8. Your office is moving to a new location.   8.____
Of the following, it would be MOST important to ensure that

    A. others will know your office's new address and phone number
    B. the new office space is comfortable
    C. your supervisor is happy with his or her new office space
    D. the move itself goes smoothly

9. Of the following, which would generally be considered the LEAST desirable?   9.____

    A. Accidentally disconnecting an executive from an important phone call
    B. Ordering the wrong back-up part for a copying machine
    C. Misplacing several hundred dollars worth of personal checks payable to your
department
    D. Misplacing a memorandum that needs to be typed

10. Your supervisor has told you not to let anyone disturb her for the rest of the morning unless absolutely necessary because she has some urgent work to complete. The department head telephones and asks to speak to her.
The BEST course of action for you to take is to

    A. ask the department head if he or she can leave a message
    B. ask your supervisor if she can take the call
    C. tell the department head that your supervisor is out
    D. let your supervisor know that her instructions have put you in a difficult position

10.____

11. Which of the following would be MOST likely to contribute to efficiency in the operation of an office?

    A. A new computer system is instituted in an office.
    B. The employees are paid well.
    C. Procedures and practices are studied for any redundant operations.
    D. A supervisor delegates work.

11.____

12. You are at work at your desk on a special project when a visitor approaches you. You cannot interrupt your work to take care of this person.
Of the following, the BEST and MOST courteous way of handling this situation is to

    A. avoid looking up from your work until you are finished with what you are doing
    B. tell the visitor that you will not be able to assist him or her for quite some time
    C. refer the individual to another employee who can take care of him or her right away
    D. chat with the individual while you continue to work

12.____

13. Which of the following would MOST likely be of the highest priority?
A(n)

    A. annual report due next month
    B. irate member of the public who is standing at your desk
    C. important financial report requested by the Commissioner
    D. memorandum to all employees outlining very important new policy needs to be typed and distributed immediately

13.____

14. Someone uses *special pull* to obtain the services of your unit at the last minute. You and the four employees you supervise have done everything you could do to provide good service, and you feel things have gone very well. The client is not pleased, however, and enters your office and begins screaming at you and the other employees present.
Of the following, it would be BEST if you

    A. ignored the person
    B. tried to calm the person down
    C. asked the person to leave the office
    D. called your supervisor in to help handle the situation

14.____

15. Your supervisor is on vacation for two weeks, and you have been asked to fill in for her.   15.____
Your office is very busy, and there is a strict procedure for filling requests. Leslie from Unit
X wants something completed immediately. You don't feel this is possible or reasonable,
and politely explain why to Leslie. Leslie becomes very angry and says that she will com-
plain to your supervisor about your uncooperative behavior as soon as your supervisor
returns.
Of the following, it would be BEST if you

    A.   filled Leslie's request
    B.   reported Leslie to her supervisor
    C.   complained to your supervisor about the situation as soon as she returned
    D.   stood by your decision once you determined it was correct

------

KEY (CORRECT ANSWERS)

1.	D	6.	B	11.	C
2.	C	7.	C	12.	C
3.	C	8.	A	13.	B
4.	C	9.	C	14.	B
5.	A	10.	B	15.	D

EXAMINATION SECTION
TEST 1

DIRECTIONS: Each question or incomplete statement is followed by several suggested answers or completions. Select the one that BEST answers the question or completes the statement. *PRINT THE LETTER OF THE CORRECT ANSWER IN THE SPACE AT THE RIGHT.*

1. Assume that a few co-workers meet near your desk and talk about personal matters during working hours. Lately, this practice has interfered with your work.
   In order to stop this practice, the BEST action for you to take FIRST is to

   A. ask your supervisor to put a stop to the co-workers' meeting near your desk
   B. discontinue any friendship with this group
   C. ask your co-workers not to meet near your desk
   D. request that your desk be moved to another location

   1.____

2. In order to maintain office coverage during working hours, your supervisor has scheduled your lunch hour from 1 P.M. to 2 P.M. and your co-worker's lunch hour from 12 P.M. to 1 P.M. Lately, your co-worker has been returning late from lunch each day. As a result, you don't get a full hour since you must return to the office by 2 P.M.
   Of the following, the BEST action for you to take FIRST is to

   A. explain to your co-worker in a courteous manner that his lateness is interfering with your right to a full hour for lunch
   B. tell your co-worker that his lateness must stop or you will report him to your supervisor
   C. report your co-worker's lateness to your supervisor
   D. leave at 1 P.M. for lunch, whether your co-worker has returned or not

   2.____

3. Assume that, as an office worker, one of your jobs is to open mail sent to your unit, read the mail for content, and send the mail to the appropriate person to handle. You accidentally open and begin to read a letter marked *personal* addressed to a co-worker.
   Of the following, the BEST action for you to take is to

   A. report to your supervisor that your co-worker is receiving personal mail at the office
   B. destroy the letter so that your co-worker does not know you saw it
   C. reseal the letter and place it on the co-worker's desk without saying anything
   D. bring the letter to your co-worker and explain that you opened it by accident

   3.____

4. Suppose that in evaluating your work, your supervisor gives you an overall good rating, but states that you sometimes turn in work with careless errors.
   The BEST action for you to take would be to

   A. ask a co-worker who is good at details to proofread your work
   B. take time to do a careful job, paying more attention to detail
   C. continue working as usual since occasional errors are to be expected
   D. ask your supervisor if she would mind correcting your errors

   4.____

5. Assume that you are taking a telephone message for a co-worker who is not in the office at the time.
   Of the following, the LEAST important item to write on the message is the

   A. length of the call   B. name of the caller
   C. time of the call   D. telephone number of the caller

   5.____

Questions 6-13.

DIRECTIONS: Questions 6 through 13 each consist of a sentence which may or may not be an example of good English. The underlined parts of each sentence may be correct or incorrect. Examine each sentence, considering grammar, punctuation, spelling, and capitalization. If the English usage in the underlined parts of the sentence given is better than any of the changes in the underlined words suggested in Options B, C, or D, choose Option A. If the changes in the underlined words suggested in Options B, C, or D would make the sentence correct, choose the correct option. Do not choose an option that will change the meaning of the sentence.

6.   This Fall, the office will be closed on Columbus Day, October 9th.   6.____

    A.   Correct as is
    B.   fall...Columbus Day, October
    C.   Fall...columbus day, October
    D.   fall...Columbus Day, october

7.   This manual discribes the duties performed by an Office Aide.   7.____

    A.   Correct as is
    B.   describe the duties performed
    C.   discribe the duties performed
    D.   describes the duties performed

8.   There weren't no paper in the supply closet.   8.____

    A.   Correct as is   B.   weren't any
    C.   wasn't any   D.   wasn't no

9.   The new employees left there office to attend a meeting.   9.____

    A.   Correct as is   B.   they're
    C.   their   D.   thier

10.   The office worker started working at 8;30 a.m.   10.____

    A.   Correct as is   B.   8:30 a.m.
    C.   8;30 a,m.   D.   8:30 am.

11.   The alphabet, or A to Z sequence are the basis of most filing systems.   11.____

    A.   Correct as is
    B.   alphabet, or A to Z sequence, is
    C.   alphabet, or A to Z sequence are
    D.   alphabet, or A too Z sequence, is

12.   Those file cabinets are five feet tall.   12.____

    A.   Correct as is   B.   Them...feet
    C.   Those...foot   D.   Them...foot

13. The Office Aide checked the <u>register and finding</u> the date of the meeting.   13._____

    A. Correct as is   B. regaster and finding
    C. register and found   D. regaster and found

Questions 14-21.

DIRECTIONS: Each of Questions 14 through 21 has two lists of numbers. Each list contains three sets of numbers. Check each of the three sets in the list on the right to see if they are the same as the corresponding set in the list on the left. Mark your answers:

    A. If none of the sets in the right list are the same as those in the left list
    B. if only one of the sets in the right list are the same as those in the left list
    C. if only two of the sets in the right list are the same as those in the left list
    D. if all three sets in the right list are the same as those in the left list

14. 7354183476   7354983476   14._____
      4474747744   4474747774
      57914302311   57914302311

15. 7143592185   7143892185   15._____
      8344517699   8344518699
      9178531263   9178531263

16. 2572114731   257214731   16._____
      8806835476   8806835476
      8255831246   8255831246

17. 331476853821   331476858621   17._____
      6976658532996   6976655832996
      3766042113715   3766042113745

18. 8806663315   8806663315   18._____
      74477138449   74477138449
      211756663666   211756663666

19. 990006966996   99000696996   19._____
      53022219743   53022219843
      4171171117717   4171171177717

20. 24400222433004   24400222433004   20._____
      5300030055000355   5300030055500355
      20000075532002022   20000075532002022

21. 61116664066000116   61116664066001116   21._____
      7111300117001100733   7111300117001100733
      26666446664476518   26666446664476518

7

Questions 22-25.

DIRECTIONS: Each of Questions 22 through 25 has two lists of names and addresses. Each list contains three sets of names and addresses. Check each of the three sets in the list on the right to see if they are the same as the corresponding set in the list on the left. Mark your answers:

    A.   if none of the sets in the right list are the same as those in the left list
    B.   if only one of the sets in the right list is the same as those in the left list
    C.   if only two of the sets in the right list are the same as those in the left list
    D.   if all three sets in the right list are the same as those in the left list

22.   Mary T. Berlinger   Mary T. Berlinger   22.____
      2351 Hampton St.   2351 Hampton St.
      Monsey, N.Y. 20117   Monsey, N.Y. 20117

      Eduardo Benes   Eduardo Benes
      473 Kingston Avenue   473 Kingston Avenue
      Central Islip, N.Y. 11734   Central Islip, N.Y. 11734

      Alan Carrington Fuchs   Alan Carrington Fuchs
      17 Gnarled Hollow Road 17 Gnarled Hollow Road
      Los Angeles, CA 91635   Los Angeles, CA 91685

23.   David John Jacobson   David John Jacobson   23.____
      178 35 St. Apt. 4C   178 53 St. Apt. 4C
      New York, N.Y. 00927   New York, N.Y. 00927

      Ann-Marie Calonella   Ann-Marie Calonella
      7243 South Ridge Blvd. 7243 South Ridge Blvd.
      Bakersfield, CA 96714   Bakersfield, CA 96714

      Pauline M. Thompson   Pauline M. Thomson
      872 Linden Ave.   872 Linden Ave.
      Houston, Texas 70321   Houston, Texas 70321

24.   Chester LeRoy Masterton Chester LeRoy Masterson 24.____
      152 Lacy Rd.   152 Lacy Rd.
      Kankakee, Ill. 54532   Kankakee, Ill. 54532

      William Maloney   William Maloney
      S. LaCrosse Pla.   S. LaCross Pla.
      Wausau, Wisconsin 52146 Wausau, Wisconsin 52146

      Cynthia V. Barnes   Cynthia V. Barnes
      16 Pines Rd.   16 Pines Rd.
      Greenpoint, Miss. 20376 Greenpoint, Miss. 20376

25. Marcel Jean Frontenac
     6 Burton On The Water
     Calender, Me. 01471

     J. Scott Marsden
     174 S. Tipton St.
     Cleveland, Ohio

     Lawrence T. Haney
     171 McDonough St.
     Decatur, Ga. 31304

Marcel Jean Frontenac
6 Burton On The Water
Calender, Me. 01471

J. Scott Marsden
174 Tipton St.
Cleveland, Ohio

Lawrence T. Haney
171 McDonough St.
Decatur, Ga. 31304

25._____

KEY (CORRECT ANSWERS)

1. C		11. B	
2. A		12. A	
3. D		13. C	
4. B		14. B	
5. A		15. B	
6. A		16. C	
7. D		17. A	
8. C		18. D	
9. C		19. A	
10. B		20. C	

21. C
22. C
23. B
24. B
25. C

TEST 2

DIRECTIONS: Each question or incomplete statement is followed by several suggested answers or completions. Select the one that BEST answers the question or completes the statement. *PRINT THE LETTER OF THE CORRECT ANSWER IN THE SPACE AT THE RIGHT.*

Questions 1-6.

DIRECTIONS: Questions 1 through 6 are to be answered SOLELY on the basis of the information contained in the following passage.

Duplicating is the process of making a number of identical copies of letters, documents, etc. from an original. Some duplicating processes make copies directly from the original document. Other duplicating processes require the preparation of a special master, and copies are then made from the master. Four of the most common duplicating processes are stencil, fluid, offset, and xerox.

In the stencil process, the typewriter is used to cut the words into a master called a stencil. Drawings, charts, or graphs can be cut into the stencil using a stylus. As many as 3,500 good-quality copies can be reproduced from one stencil. Various grades of finished paper from inexpensive mimeograph to expensive bond can be used.

The fluid process is a good method of copying from 50 to 125 good-quality copies from a master, which is prepared with a special dye. The master is placed on the duplicator, and special paper with a hard finish is moistened and then passed through the duplicator. Some of the dye on the master is dissolved, creating an impression on the paper. The impression becomes lighter as more copies are made; and once the dye on the master is used up, a new master must be made.

The offset process is the most adaptable office duplicating process because this process can be used for making a few copies or many copies. Masters can be made on paper or plastic for a few hundred copies, or on metal plates for as many as 75,000 copies. By using a special technique called photo-offset, charts, photographs, illustrations, or graphs can be reproduced on the master plate. The offset process is capable of producing large quantities of fine, top-quality copies on all types of finished paper.

The xerox process reproduces an exact duplicate from an original. It is the fastest duplicating method because the original material is placed directly on the duplicator, eliminating the need to make a special master. Any kind of paper can be used. The xerox process is the most expensive duplicating process; however, it is the best method of reproducing small quantities of good-quality copies of reports, letters, official documents, memos, or contracts.

1. Of the following, the MOST efficient method of reproducing 5,000 copies of a graph is   1._____

    A. stencil   B. fluid   C. offset   D. xerox

2. The offset process is the MOST adaptable office duplicating process because   2._____

    A. it is the quickest duplicating method
    B. it is the least expensive duplicating method
    C. it can produce a small number or large number of copies
    D. a softer master can be used over and over again

3. Which one of the following duplicating processes uses moistened paper?   3.____

    A. Stencil   B. Fluid   C. Offset   D. Xerox

4. The fluid process would be the BEST process to use for reproducing   4.____

    A. five copies of a school transcript
    B. fifty copies of a memo
    C. five hundred copies of a form letter
    D. five thousand copies of a chart

5. Which one of the following duplicating processes does NOT require a special master?   5.____

    A. Fluid   B. Xerox   C. Offset   D. Stencil

6. Xerox is NOT used for all duplicating jobs because   6.____

    A. it produces poor-quality copies
    B. the process is too expensive
    C. preparing the master is too time-consuming
    D. it cannot produce written reports

7. Assume a city agency has 775 office workers.   7.____
If 2 out of 25 office workers were absent on a particular day, how many office workers reported to work on that day?

    A. 713   B. 744   C. 750   D. 773

Questions 8-11.

DIRECTIONS: In Questions 8 through 11, select the choice that is CLOSEST in meaning to the underlined word.

SAMPLE: This division reviews the fiscal reports of the agency.
      In this sentence, the word fiscal means MOST NEARLY
       A. financial   B. critical   C. basic   D. personnel

      The correct answer is A, financial, because financial is closest to fiscal.

8. A central file eliminates the need to retain duplicate material.   8.____
The word retain means MOST NEARLY

    A. keep   B. change   C. locate   D. process

9. Filing is a routine office task.   9.____
Routine means MOST NEARLY

    A. proper   B. regular   C. simple   D. difficult

10. Sometimes a word, phrase, or sentence must be deleted to correct an error.   10.____
Deleted means MOST NEARLY

    A. removed   B. added   C. expanded   D. improved

11. Your supervisor will <u>evaluate</u> your work. 11._____
    <u>Evaluate</u> means MOST NEARLY

    A. judge   B. list   C. assign   D. explain

Questions 12-19.

DIRECTIONS: The code table below shows 10 letters with matching numbers. For each
              Question 12 through 19, there are three sets of letters. Each set of letters is
              followed by a set of numbers which may or may not match their correct letter
              according to the code table. For each question, check all three sets of letters
              and numbers and mark your answer:
              A. if no pairs are correctly matched
              B. if only one pair is correctly matched
              C. if only two pairs are correctly matched
              D. if all three pairs are correctly matched

CODE TABLE

T	M	V	D	S	P	R	G	B	H
1	2	3	4	5	6	7	8	9	0

<u>Sample Question:</u>   TMVDSP - 123456
                          RGBHTM - 789011
                          DSPRGB - 256789

In the sample question above, the first set of numbers correctly matches its set of letters. But
the second and third pairs contain mistakes. In the second pair, M is incorrectly matched with
number 1. According to the code table, letter M should be correctly matched with number 2. In
the third pair, the letter D is incorrectly matched with number 2. According to the code table, letter D should be correctly matched with number 4. Since only one of the pairs is correctly
matched, the answer to this sample question is B.

12. RSBMRM - 759262   12._____
    GDSRVH - 845730
    VDBRTM - 349713

13. TGVSDR - 183247   13._____
    SMHRDP - 520647
    TRMHSR - 172057

14. DSPRGM - 456782   14._____
    MVDBHT - 234902
    HPMDBT - 062491

15. BVPTRD - 936184   15._____
    GDPHMB - 807029
    GMRHMV - 827032

16. MGVRSH - 283750   16._____
    TRDMBS - 174295
    SPRMGV - 567283

17. SGBSDM - 489542
     MGHPTM - 290612
     MPBMHT - 269301

17._____

18. TDPBHM - 146902
     VPBMRS - 369275
     GDMBHM - 842902

18._____

19. MVPTBV - 236194
     PDRTMB - 647128
     BGTMSM - 981232

19._____

Questions 20-25.

DIRECTIONS: In each of Questions 20 through 25, the names of four people are given. For each question, choose as your answer the one of the four names given which should be filed FIRST according to the usual system of alphabetical filing of names, as described in the following paragraph.

In filing names, you must start with the last name. Names are filed in order of the first letter of the last name, then the second letter, etc. Therefore, BAILY would be filed before BROWN, which would be filed before COLT. A name with fewer letters of the same type comes first; i.e., Smith before Smithe. If the last names are the same, the names are filed alphabetically by the first name. If the first name is an initial, a name with an initial would come before a first name that starts with the same letter as the initial. Therefore, I. BROWN would come before IRA BROWN. Finally, if both last name and first name are the same, the name would be filed alphabetically by the middle name, one again an initial coming before a middle name which starts with the same letter as the initial. If there is no middle name at all, the name would come before those with middle initials or names.

Sample Question: A. Lester Daniels
                   B. William Dancer
                   C. Nathan Danzig
                   D. Dan Lester

The last names beginning with D are filed before the last name beginning with L. Since DANIELS, DANCER, and DANZIG all begin with the same three letters, you must look at the fourth letter of the last name to determine which name should be filed first. C comes before I or Z in the alphabet, so DANCER is filed before DANIELS or DANZIG. Therefore, the answer to the above sample question is B.

20. A. Scott Biala   B. Mary Byala   20._____
     C. Martin Baylor   D. Francis Bauer

21. A. Howard J. Black   B. Howard Black   21._____
     C. J. Howard Black   D. John H. Black

22. A. Theodora Garth Kingston   B. Theadore Barth Kingston   22._____
     C. Thomas Kingston   D. Thomas T. Kingston

23. A. Paulette Mary Huerta   B. Paul M. Huerta   23._____
     C. Paulette L. Huerta   D. Peter A. Huerta

24. A. Martha Hunt Morgan   B. Martin Hunt Morgan   24.____
     C. Mary H. Morgan   D. Martine H. Morgan

25. A. James T. Meerschaum   B. James M. Mershum   25.____
     C. James F. Mearshaum   D. James N. Meshum

———

KEY (CORRECT ANSWERS)

1.	C	11.	A
2.	C	12.	B
3.	B	13.	B
4.	B	14.	C
5.	B	15.	A
6.	B	16.	D
7.	A	17.	A
8.	A	18.	D
9.	B	19.	A
10.	A	20.	D

21.	B
22.	B
23.	B
24.	A
25.	C

———

TEST 3

Each question or incomplete statement is followed by several suggested answers or completions. Select the one that BEST answers the question or completes the statement. *PRINT THE LETTER OF THE CORRECT ANSWER IN THE SPACE AT THE RIGHT.*

1. Which one of the following statements about proper telephone usage is NOT always cor-   1.____
rect?
   When answering the telephone, you should

   A. know whom you are speaking to
   B. give the caller your undivided attention
   C. identify yourself to the caller
   D. obtain the information the caller wishes before you do your other work

2. Assume that, as a member of a worker's safety committee in your agency, you are   2.____
responsible for encouraging other employees to follow correct safety practices. While you
are working on your regular assignment, you observe an employee violating a safety
rule.
   Of the following, the BEST action for you to take FIRST is to

   A. speak to the employee about safety practices and order him to stop violating the
       safety rule
   B. speak to the employee about safety practices and point out the safety rule he is
       violating
   C. bring the matter up in the next committee meeting
   D. report this violation of the safety rule to the employee's supervisor

3. Assume that you have been temporarily assigned by your supervisor to do a job which   3.____
you do not want to do. The BEST action for you to take is to

   A. discuss the job with your supervisor, explaining why you do not want to do it
   B. discuss the job with your supervisor and tell her that you will not do it
   C. ask a co-worker to take your place on this job
   D. do some other job that you like; your supervisor may give the job you do not like to
       someone else

4. Assume that you keep the confidential personnel files of employees in your unit. A friend   4.____
asks you to obtain some information from the file of one of your co-workers.
   The BEST action to take is to _____ to your friend.

   A. ask the co-worker if you can give the information
   B. ask your supervisor if you can give the information
   C. give the information
   D. refuse to give the information

Questions 5-8.

DIRECTIONS: Questions 5 through 8 are to be answered SOLELY on the basis of the information contained in the following passage.

City government is committed to providing a safe and healthy work environment for all city employees. An effective agency safety program reduces accidents by educating employees about the types of careless acts which can cause accidents. Even in an office, accidents can happen. If each employee is aware of possible safety hazards, the number of accidents on the job can be reduced.

Careless use of office equipment can cause accidents and injuries. For example, file cabinet drawers which are filled with papers can be so heavy that the entire cabinet could tip over from the weight of one open drawer.

The bottom drawers of desks and file cabinets should never be left open since employees could easily trip over open drawers and injure themselves.

When reaching for objects on a high shelf, an employee should use a strong, sturdy object such as a step stool to stand on. Makeshift platforms made out of books, papers, or boxes can easily collapse. Even chairs can slide out from under foot, causing serious injury.

Even at an employee's desk, safety hazards can occur. Frayed or cut wires should be repaired or replaced immediately. Computers which are not firmly anchored to the desk or table could fall, causing injury.

Smoking is one of the major causes of fires in the office. A lighted match or improperly extinguished cigarette thrown into a wastebasket filled with paper could cause a major fire with possible loss of life. Where smoking is permitted, ashtrays should be used. Smoking is particularly dangerous in offices where flammable chemicals are used.

5. The goal of an effective safety program is to   5.____

    A. reduce office accidents
    B. stop employees from smoking on the job
    C. encourage employees to continue their education
    D. eliminate high shelves in offices

6. Desks and file cabinets can become safety hazards when   6.____

    A. their drawers are left open
    B. they are used as wastebaskets
    C. they are makeshift
    D. they are not anchored securely to the floor

7. Smoking is especially hazardous when it occurs   7.____

    A. near exposed wires
    B. in a crowded office
    C. in an area where flammable chemicals are used
    D. where books and papers are stored

8. Accidents are likely to occur when   8.____

    A. employees' desks are cluttered with books and papers
    B. employees are not aware of safety hazards
    C. employees close desk drawers
    D. step stools are used to reach high objects

9. Assume that part of your job as a worker in the accounting division of a city agency is to answer the telephone. When you first answer the telephone, it is LEAST important to tell the caller

    A. your title   B. your name
    C. the name of your unit   D. the name of your agency

    9._____

10. Assume that you are assigned to work as a receptionist, and your duties are to answer phones, greet visitors, and do other general office work. You are busy with a routine job when several visitors approach your desk.
The BEST action to take is to

    A. ask the visitors to have a seat and assist them after your work is completed
    B. tell the visitors that you are busy and they should return at a more convenient time
    C. stop working long enough to assist the visitors
    D. continue working and wait for the visitors to ask you for assistance

    10._____

11. Assume that your supervisor has chosen you to take a special course during working hours to learn a new payroll procedure. Although you know that you were chosen because of your good work record, a co-worker, who feels that he should have been chosen, has been telling everyone in your unit that the choice was unfair.
Of the following, the BEST way to handle this situation FIRST is to

    A. suggest to the co-worker that everything in life is unfair
    B. contact your union representative in case your co-worker presents a formal grievance
    C. tell your supervisor about your co-worker's complaints and let her handle the situation
    D. tell the co-worker that you were chosen because of your superior work record

    11._____

12. Assume that while you are working on an assignment which must be completed quickly, a supervisor from another unit asks you to obtain information for her.
Of the following, the BEST way to respond to her request is to

    A. tell her to return in an hour since you are busy
    B. give her the names of some people in her own unit who could help her
    C. tell her you are busy and refer her to a co-worker
    D. tell her that you are busy and ask her if she could wait until you finish your assignment

    12._____

13. A co-worker in your unit is often off from work because of illness. Your supervisor assigns the co-worker's work to you when she is not there. Lately, doing her work has interfered with your own job.
The BEST action for you to take FIRST is to

    A. discuss the problem with your supervisor
    B. complete your own work before starting your co-worker's work
    C. ask other workers in your unit to assist you
    D. work late in order to get the jobs done

    13._____

14. During the month of June, 40,587 people attended a city-owned swimming pool. In July, 13,014 more people attended the swimming pool than the number that had attended in June. In August, 39,655 people attended the swimming pool.
The TOTAL number of people who attended the swimming pool during the months of June, July, and August was

14._____

    A. 80,242   B. 93,256   C. 133,843   D. 210,382

Questions 15-22.

DIRECTIONS: Questions 15 through 22 test how well you understand what you read. It will be necessary for you to read carefully because your answers to these questions must be based ONLY on the information in the following paragraphs.

The telephone directory is made up of two books. The first book consists of the introductory section and the alphabetical listing of names section. The second book is the classified directory (also known as the yellow pages). Many people who are familiar with one book do not realize how useful the other can be. The efficient office worker should become familiar with both books in order to make the best use of this important source of information.

The introductory section gives general instructions for finding numbers in the alphabetical listing and classified directory. This section also explains how to use the telephone company's many services, including the operator and information services, gives examples of charges for local and long-distance calls, and lists area codes for the entire country. In addition, this section provides a useful postal zip code map.

The alphabetical listing of names section lists the names, addresses, and telephone numbers of subscribers in an area. Guide names, or *telltales,* are on the top corner of each page. These guide names indicate the first and last name to be found on that page. *Telltales* help locate any particular name quickly. A cross-reference spelling is also given to help locate names which are spelled several different ways. City, state, and federal government agencies are listed under the major government heading. For example, an agency of the federal government would be listed under *United States Government.*

The classified directory, or yellow pages, is a separate book. In this section are advertising services, public transportation line maps, shopping guides, and listings of businesses arranged by the type of product or services they offer. This book is most useful when looking for the name or phone number of a business when all that is known is the type of product offered and the address, or when trying to locate a particular type of business in an area. Businesses listed in the classified directory can usually be found in the alphabetical listing of names section. When the name of the business is known, you will find the address or phone number more quickly in the alphabetical listing of names section.

15. The introductory section provides

15._____

    A. shopping guides   B. government listings
    C. business listings   D. information services

16. Advertising services would be found in the

16._____

    A. introductory section   B. alphabetical listing of names section
    C. classified directory   D. information services

17. According to the information in the above passage for locating government agencies, the   17._____
Information Office of the Department of Consumer Affairs of New York City government
would be alphabetically listed FIRST under

    A. *I* for Information Offices
    B. *D* for Department of Consumer Affairs
    C. *N* for New York City
    D. *G* for government

18. When the name of a business is known, the QUICKEST way to find the phone number is   18.____
to look in the

    A. classified directory
    B. introductory section
    C. alphabetical listing of names section
    D. advertising service section

19. The QUICKEST way to find the phone number of a business when the type of service a   19._____
business offers and its address is known is to look in the

    A. classified directory
    B. alphabetical listing of names section
    C. introductory section
    D. information service

20. What is a *telltale?*   20._____

    A. An alphabetical listing
    B. A guide name
    C. A map
    D. A cross-reference listing

21. The BEST way to find a postal zip code is to look in the   21._____

    A. classified directory
    B. introductory section
    C. alphabetical listing of names section
    D. government heading

22. To help find names which have several different spellings, the telephone directory pro-   22._____
vides

    A. cross-reference spelling   B. *telltales*
    C. spelling guides   D. advertising services

23. Assume that your agency has been given $2025 to purchase file cabinets.   23._____
If each file cabinet costs $135, how many file cabinets can your agency purchase?

    A. 8   B. 10   C. 15   D. 16

24. Assume that your unit ordered 14 staplers at a total cost of $30.20, and each stapler cost   24.____
the same.
The cost of one stapler was MOST NEARLY

    A. $1.02   B. $1.61   C. $2.16   D. $2.26

25. Assume that you are responsible for counting and recording licensing fees collected by   25.____
your department. On a particular day, your department collected in fees 40 checks in the
amount of $6 each, 80 checks in the amount of $4 each, 45 twenty dollar bills, 30 ten dollar bills, 42 five dollar bills, and 186 one dollar bills.
The TOTAL amount in fees collected on that day was

    A. $1,406   B. $1,706   C. $2,156   D. $2,356

26. Assume that you are responsible for your agency's petty cash fund. During the month of   26.____
February, you pay out 7 $2.00 subway fares and one taxi fare for $10.85. You pay out
nothing else from the fund. At the end of February, you count the money left in the fund
and find 3 one dollar bills, 4 quarters, 5 dimes, and 4 nickels. The amount of money you
had available in the petty cash fund at the BEGINNING of February was

    A. $4.70   B. $16.35   C. $24.85   D. $29.55

27. You overhear your supervisor criticize a co-worker for handling equipment in an unsafe   27.____
way. You feel that the criticism may be unfair.
Of the following, it would be BEST for you to

    A. take your co-worker aside and tell her how you feel about your supervisor's com-
ments
    B. interrupt the discussion and defend your co-worker to your supervisor
    C. continue working as if you had not overheard the discussion
    D. make a list of other workers who have violated safety rules and give it to your
supervisor

28. Assume that you have been assigned to work on a long-term project with an employee   28.____
who is known for being uncooperative.
In beginning to work with this employee, it would be LEAST desirable for you to

    A. understand why the person is uncooperative
    B. act in a calm manner rather than an emotional manner
    C. be appreciative of the co-worker's work
    D. report the co-worker's lack of cooperation to your supervisor

29. Assume that you are assigned to sell tickets at a city-owned ice skating rink. An adult   29.____
ticket costs $4.50, and a children's ticket costs $2.25. At the end of a day, you find that
you have sold 36 adult tickets and 80 children's tickets.
The TOTAL amount of money you collected for that day was

    A. $244.80   B. $318.00   C. $342.00   D. $348.00

30. If each office worker files 487 index cards in one hour, how many cards can 26 office   30.____
workers file in one hour?

    A. 10,662   B. 12,175   C. 12,662   D. 14,266

KEY (CORRECT ANSWERS)

1.	D	16.	C
2.	B	17.	C
3.	A	18.	C
4.	D	19.	A
5.	A	20.	B
6.	A	21.	B
7.	C	22.	A
8.	B	23.	C
9.	A	24.	C
10.	C	25.	C
11.	C	26.	D
12.	D	27.	C
13.	A	28.	D
14.	C	29.	C
15.	D	30.	C

———

EXAMINATION SECTION
TEST 1

DIRECTIONS: Each question or incomplete statement is followed by several suggested answers or completions. Select the one that BEST answers the question or completes the statement. *PRINT THE LETTER OF THE CORRECT ANSWER IN THE SPACE AT THE RIGHT.*

1. Assume that you are appointed as a clerk in a city department. As a new employee, you are PRIMARILY expected to   1.____

    A. inform your supervisor of the amount of training you will need to handle your new job
    B. perform your work in accordance with the instructions given you by your supervisor
    C. show your supervisor that you like the work you are assigned to do
    D. prove to your supervisor that you are able to handle your new job with very little instruction

2. Assume that you are a clerk in a city agency. One day, your supervisor tells you that he will be too busy to speak to visitors coming to the office that day. He instructs you to refer all visitors, including those with urgent business, to Mr. Brown, one of his assistants. During the day, a visitor enters the office and tells you that he wishes to speak to your supervisor on an important matter. Of the following, the MOST appropriate course of action for you to take in this situation is to   2.____

    A. advise the visitor that Mr. Brown may be better informed than your supervisor on the matter
    B. notify your supervisor that a visitor wishes to speak to him on an important matter
    C. ask the visitor to return at another time when your supervisor will be able to speak to him
    D. inform the visitor that your supervisor is not available but that Mr. Brown will attempt to help him

3. As a clerk in the mail room of a large city department, you are responsible for opening incoming letters and for routing them to the appropriate offices in the department. The MOST important reason why you should know thoroughly the functions of the various offices in the department is that   3.____

    A. letters are sometimes addressed only to the department rather than to a specific office in the department
    B. each office may have its own method of answering letters
    C. a letter addressed only to the department would not have to be opened before forwarding it to the proper office
    D. an accurate listing of the locations of offices and employees in the department is essential to a mail room clerk

4. Suppose that one of your duties as a clerk in a city department is to answer letters requesting information. One such letter requests some information that you can supply immediately and other information which you know will not be available for several weeks. It is evident that the writer of the letter is not aware that some of the information is not available immediately.
Of the following, the MOST appropriate action for you to take in this matter is to   4.____

    A.   supply the writer with the information that is available immediately and ask him to write for the rest of the information at a later date

    B.   supply the writer with the information that is available immediately and inform him that the rest of the information will be sent in several weeks

    C.   write to the person requesting the information, asking him to make his request again in several weeks when all the information will be available

    D.   wait until the rest of the information becomes available in several weeks and then send all the information at once

5.   Assume that you have been given an unalphabetized list of 1,000 employees in your agency and a set of unalphabetized payroll cards. You have been asked to determine if, for each name on the list, there is a corresponding payroll card.
   Of the following, the BEST reason for first alphabetizing the payroll cards is that   5.____

    A.   each name on the list could then be more easily checked against the payroll cards

    B.   it then becomes easier to alphabetize the names on the list

    C.   introducing an additional step in the checking process produces a more compli-cated procedure

    D.   you may obtain additional information from the payroll cards to help you check the names

6.   Suppose that you have just been appointed as a clerk in a city department. Although your supervisor has given you instructions for filing personnel cards, you still do not fully understand how to file them.
   For you to ask your supervisor to explain more fully how you are to file the cards would be desirable CHIEFLY because   6.____

    A.   you will prove to your supervisor that you intend to do a good job

    B.   your supervisor will be willing to explain the instructions more fully

    C.   you will be better prepared to do the assignment if you fully understand what you are to do

    D.   new employees cannot be expected to do their work properly without having instructions repeated

7.   In many cases, it becomes evident that a filing problem exists only after a paper has been filed and cannot be found.
   On the basis of the above statement, it is MOST accurate to state that   7.____

    A.   filing problems become evident before errors in filing have been discovered

    B.   a filing problem is solved when a misfiled paper is found

    C.   even a careful file clerk may create a filing problem

    D.   a filing problem may not become apparent until a filed paper cannot be located

8.   Assume that you are a newly appointed clerk in a large office of a city department. You believe that the method used for doing a certain type of work in the office should be changed.
   Of the following, the MOST important reason why you should suggest the change to your supervisor is that   8.____

    A.   supervisors are usually reluctant to make changes unless they are necessary

    B.   you are expected, as a new employee, to suggest important improvements in office work

C. your suggestion may improve the method used for this type of work
D. it is more important to make changes in large offices than in small ones

9. The average citizen is not interested in the amount of work assigned to public employees or the pressure under which they sometimes work. If a public employee fails to give prompt and courteous service, the average citizen estimates the efficiency of all public employees accordingly.
On the basis of the above passage, the MOST accurate of the following statements is that

    A. the average citizen usually realizes that the efficiency of public employees depends upon the amount of work assigned to them
    B. the average citizen's attitude toward all public employees may be influenced by the service rendered by an individual public employee
    C. the pressure of work duties often causes public employees to render unsatisfactory service to the public
    D. the average citizen may help to improve the efficiency of public employees by taking an interest in their work

9.____

10. Suppose that you have been asked to proofread a copy of a report with another clerk. The other clerk is to read to you from the original report while you check the copy for errors.
For you to make a notation of each error as you detect it rather than wait until the end of the proofreading to note all the errors at once would be

    A. *desirable;* you would be less likely to overlook noting an error
    B. *undesirable;* the original report may not be correct
    C. *desirable;* the more clearly the other clerk reads, the more accurately you will be able to detect and note errors
    D. *undesirable;* the notations made during the proofreading may not be legible later

10.____

11. If the methods used in an office seem to be faulty, an employee should offer constructive suggestions instead of mere criticisms of the methods.
On the basis of this statement, it is MOST accurate to state that

    A. the methods used in an office should be criticized only if they cannot be improved
    B. most of the problems arising in an office can be overcome satisfactorily by employee suggestions
    C. an employee should suggest improvements for existing poor methods rather than only find fault with them
    D. the quality of suggestions submitted by employees depends upon the methods used in an office

11.____

12. The abbreviation *e.g.* ORDINARILY means

    A. instead of
    C. for example
    B. express charges guaranteed
    D. excellent grade

12.____

13. As a clerk assigned to keeping payroll records in your department, you are instructed by your supervisor to use a new method for keeping the records. You think that the new method will be less effective than the one you are now using.
In this situation, it would be MOST advisable for you to

13.____

A. use the new method to keep the records even if you think it may be less effective
B. continue to use the method you consider to be more effective without saying any-thing to your supervisor
C. use the method you consider to be more effective and then tell your supervisor your reasons for doing so
D. use the new method only if you can improve its effectiveness

14. The term that describes the programs installed on an office computer is   14.____

   A. interface   B. hardware
   C. network   D. software

15. An examination of the financial records of a business firm or public agency in order to   15.____
   determine its true financial condition is called a(n)

   A. budget   B. voucher
   C. audit   D. appropriation

Questions 16-17.

DIRECTIONS: Questions 16 and 17 are to be answered SOLELY on the basis of the informa-tion contained in the following statement.

   A duplex envelope is an envelope composed of two sections securely fastened together so that they become one mailing piece. This type of envelope makes it possible for a first class letter to be delivered simultaneously with third or fourth class matter and yet not require payment of the much higher first class postage rate on the entire mailing. First class postage is paid only on the letter which goes in the small compartment, third or fourth class postage being paid on the contents of the larger compartment. The larger compartment generally has an ungummed flap or clasp for sealing. The first class or smaller compartment has a gummed flap for sealing. Postal regulations require that the exact amount of postage applicable to each compartment be separately attached to it.

16. On the basis of this paragraph, it is MOST accurate to state that   16.____

   A. the smaller compartment is placed inside the larger compartment before mailing
   B. the two compartments may be detached and mailed separately
   C. two classes of mailing matter may be mailed as a unit at two different postage rates
   D. the more expensive postage rate is paid on the matter in the larger compartment

17. When a duplex envelope is used, the   17.____

   A. first class compartment may be sealed with a clasp
   B. correct amount of postage must be placed on each compartment
   C. compartment containing third or fourth class mail requires a gummed flap for seal-ing
   D. full amount of postage for both compartments may be placed on the larger com-partment

18. The MOST accurate of the following statements is that a City Charter   18.____

   A. lists the names, titles, and salaries of the heads of the various city agencies
   B. shows the funds allocated to each city agency

C. contains all the local laws passed by the City Council
D. describes the functions of city agencies

19. A period of inflation may generally BEST be described as a period in which the   19.____

A. hourly and weekly wages paid to employees decline rapidly
B. purchasing power of pensions and other fixed incomes increases
C. purchasing power of money declines
D. number of unemployed persons increases sharply

20. You have been asked by your supervisor to code about 500 cards on each of six different   20.____
classification bases according to a previously prepared key. Halfway through the task,
you realize suddenly that on the last few cards, you have begun to use incorrect code
numbers in coding one particular classification. You know that your work will be checked
by another clerk.
For you to go back to the beginning of the cards immediately and to check the coding
of only the particular classification in the coding of which you have erred would be
commendable CHIEFLY because

A. all the cards will be checked carefully by another clerk
B. you have probably misinterpreted the entire coding key
C. there is an especially strong likelihood of error in the coding of the particular classi-
fication
D. you have almost completed the task and no time will be wasted

21. Suppose that it is the practice in your department to file all the correspondence with one   21.____
individual in a single folder and to file the most recent letters first in the folder.
Of the following, the BEST justification for placing the most recent letter first rather than
last in the folder is that, in general,

A. letters placed in front of a folder are usually less accessible
B. requests for previous correspondence from the files usually concern letters filed
relatively recently
C. letters in a folder can usually be located most quickly when they are filed in a definite order
D. filing can usually be accomplished very quickly when letters are placed in a folder
without reference to date

22. While filing cards in an alphabetical file, you notice a card which is not in its correct   22.____
alphabetical order.
Of the following, the BEST action for you to take is to

A. show the card to your supervisor and ask him whether that card has been reported
lost
B. leave the card where it is, but inform the other clerks who use the file exactly where
they may find the card if they need it
C. file a cross-reference card in the place where the card should have been filed
D. make a written notation of where you can find the card in the event that your supervisor asks you for it

23. The sum of 637.894, 8352.16, 4.8673, and 301.5 is MOST NEARLY   23.____

A. 8989.5   B. 9021.35   C. 9294.9   D. 9296.4

24. If 30 is divided by .06, the result is　　　　　　　　　　　　　　　　24.____

    A.　5　　　　　　B.　5　　　　　　C.　500　　　　　　D.　5000

25. The sum of the fractions 1/3, 4/6, 1/2, 3/4 and 1/12 is　　　　　　25.____

    A.　3 1/4　　　　B.　2 1/3　　　　C.　2 1/6　　　　D.　1 11/12

26. If 96934.42 is divided by 53.496, the result is MOST NEARLY　　　26.____

    A.　181　　　　　B.　552　　　　　C.　1810　　　　D.　5520

27. If 25% of a number is 48, the number is　　　　　　　　　　　　　27.____

    A.　12　　　　　　B.　60　　　　　　C.　144　　　　　D.　192

28. The average number of reports filed per day by a clerk during a five-day week was 720.　28.____
He filed 610 reports the first day, 720 reports the second day, 740 reports the third day,
and 755 reports the fourth day.
The number of reports he filed the fifth day was

    A.　748　　　　　B.　165　　　　　C.　775　　　　　D.　565

29. The number 88 is 2/5 of　　　　　　　　　　　　　　　　　　　　29.____

    A.　123　　　　　B.　141　　　　　C.　220　　　　　D.　440

30. If the product of 8.3 multiplied by .42 is subtracted from the product of 156 multiplied by　30.____
.09, the result is MOST NEARLY

    A.　10.6　　　　B.　13.7　　　　C.　17.5　　　　D.　20.8

31. A city department employs 1400 people, of whom 35% are clerks and 1/8 are stenogra-　31.____
phers.
The number of employees in the department who are neither clerks nor stenographers
is

    A.　640　　　　　B.　665　　　　　C.　735　　　　　D.　760

32. Assume that there are 190 papers to be filed and that Clerk A and Clerk B are assigned　32.____
to file these papers. If Clerk A files 40 papers more than Clerk B, then the number of
papers that Clerk A files is

    A.　75　　　　　　B.　110　　　　　C.　115　　　　　D.　150

33. A stock clerk had on hand the following items:　　　　　　　　　　33.____
500　pads, each worth four cents
130　pencils, each worth three cents
 50　dozen rubber bands, worth two cents a dozen
If, from this stock, he issued 125 pads, 45 pencils, and 48 rubber bands, the value of
the remaining stock would be

    A.　$6.43　　　　B.　$8.95　　　　C.　$17.63　　　　D.　$18.47

34. An assignment is completed by 32 clerks in 22 days. Assuming that all the clerks work at　34.____
the same rate of speed, the number of clerks that would be needed to complete this
assignment in 16 days is

A. 27   B. 38   C. 44   D. 52

35. A department head hired a total of 60 temporary employees to handle a seasonal increase in the department's workload. The following lists the number of temporary employees hired, their rates of pay, and the duration of their employment:
One-third of the total were hired as clerks, each at the rate of $13,750 a year, for two months
30 percent of the total were hired as office machine operators, each at the rate of $15,750 a year, for four months
22 stenographers were hired, each at the rate of $15,000 a year, for three months
The total amount paid to these temporary employees was MOST NEARLY

35.____

A. $890,000   B. $225,000   C. $325,000   D. $196,000

36. Assume that there are 2300 employees in a city agency. Also assume that five percent of these employees are accountants, that 80 percent of the accountants have college degrees, and that one-half of the accountants who have college degrees have five years of experience.
Then the number of employees in the agency who are accountants with college degrees and five years of experience is

36.____

A. 46   B. 51   C. 460   D. 920

Questions 37-50.

DIRECTIONS: Each of Questions 37 to 50 consists of a word in capitals followed by four suggested meanings of the word. For each question, indicate in the correspondingly numbered space at the right the letter preceding the word which means MOST NEARLY the same as the word in capitals.

37. AUXILIARY

37.____

A. unofficial   B. available   C. temporary   D. aiding

38. DELETE

38.____

A. explain   B. delay   C. erase   D. conceal

39. REFUTE

39.____

A. receive   B. endorse   C. disprove   D. decline

40. CANDID

40.____

A. correct   B. hasty   C. careful   D. frank

41. INFRACTION

41.____

A. violation   B. investigation   C. punishment   D. part

42. OBJECTIVE

42.____

A. method   B. goal   C. importance   D. fault

43. CONCUR

43.____

A. agree   B. demand   C. control   D. create

44. JUSTIFY   44.___
    A. defend   B. understand   C. complete   D. request

45. INFER   45.___
    A. impress   B. conclude   C. intrude   D. decrease

46. CONSTRUE   46.___
    A. suggest   B. predict   C. interpret   D. urge

47. TRIVIAL   47.___
    A. unexpected   B. exact   C. unnecessary   D. petty

48. OPTIONAL   48.___
    A. useful   B. voluntary   C. valuable   D. obvious

49. SUBSEQUENT   49.___
    A. following   B. successful   C. permanent   D. simple

50. REVISE   50.___
    A. introduce   B. explain   C. begin   D. change

KEY (CORRECT ANSWERS)

1. B	11. C	21. B	31. C	41. A
2. D	12. C	22. A	32. C	42. B
3. A	13. A	23. D	33. D	43. A
4. B	14. D	24. C	34. C	44. A
5. A	15. C	25. B	35. B	45. B
6. C	16. C	26. C	36. A	46. C
7. D	17. B	27. D	37. D	47. D
8. C	18. D	28. C	38. C	48. B
9. B	19. C	29. C	39. C	49. A
10. A	20. C	30. A	40. D	50. D

TEST 2

DIRECTIONS: Each of Questions 1 to 9 consists of a word in capitals followed by four suggested meanings of the word. For each question, indicate in the correspondingly numbered space at the right the letter preceding the word which means MOST NEARLY the same as the word in capitals.

1. CONCISE   1.____
   A. hidden   B. complicated   C. compact   D. recent

2. PROSPECTIVE   2.____
   A. anticipated   B. patient   C. influential   D. shrewd

3. STIMULATE   3.____
   A. regulate   B. arouse   C. imitate   D. strengthen

4. EXPEDITE   4.____
   A. exceed   B. expand   C. solve   D. hasten

5. RENOUNCE   5.____
   A. remind   B. raise   C. reject   D. restore

6. SURMISE   6.____
   A. inform   B. suppose   C. convince   D. pretend

7. FLUCTUATE   7.____
   A. vary   B. divide   C. improve   D. irritate

8. PERTINENT   8.____
   A. attractive   B. related   C. practical   D. lasting

9. CENSURE   9.____
   A. confess   B. count   C. confirm   D. criticize

Questions 10-14.

DIRECTIONS: Each of Questions 10 to 14 consists of a sentence which may be classified appropriately under one of the following four categories:
   A. incorrect because of faulty grammar or sentence structure
   B. incorrect because of faulty punctuation
   C. incorrect because of faulty capitalization
   D. correct

Examine each sentence carefully. Then, in the correspondingly numbered space at the right, indicate the letter preceding the category which is the BEST of the four suggested above. Each incorrect sentence contains only one type of error. Consider a sentence correct if it contains none of the types of errors mentioned, although there may be other correct ways of expressing the same thought.

10. We have learned that there was more than twelve people present at the meeting.   10.___

11. Every one of the employees is able to do this kind of work.   11.___

12. Neither the supervisor nor his assistant are in the office today.   12.___

13. The office manager announced that any clerk, who volunteered for the assignment, would be rewarded.   13.___

14. After looking carefully in all the files, the letter was finally found on a desk.   14.___

15. In answer to the clerk's question, the supervisor said, "this assignment must be completed today."   15.___

16. The office manager says that he can permit only you and me to go to the meeting.   16.___

17. The supervisor refused to state who he would assign to the reception unit.   17.___

18. At the last meeting, he said that he would interview us in September.   18.___

19. Mr. Jones, who is one of our most experienced employees has been placed in charge of the main office.   19.___

20. I think that this adding machine is the most useful of the two we have in our office.   20.___

21. Between you and I, our new stenographer is not as competent as our former stenographer.   21.___

22. The new assignment should be given to whoever can do the work rapidly.   22.___

23. Mrs. Smith, as well as three other typists, was assigned to the new office.   23.___

24. The staff assembled for the conference on time but, the main speaker arrived late.   24.___

Questions 25-34.

DIRECTIONS: Each of Questions 25 to 34 consists of a group of four words. One word in each group is INCORRECTLY spelled. For each question, indicate in the correspondingly numbered space at the right the letter preceding the word which is INCORRECTLY spelled.

25.   A. arguing   B. correspon-dance   C. forfeit   D. dissension   25.__

26.   A. occasion   B. description   C. prejudice   D. elegible   26.__

27.   A. accomodate   B. initiative   C. changeable   D. enroll   27.__

28.   A. temporary   B. insistent   C. benificial   D. separate   28.__

29.   A. achieve   B. dissappoint   C. unanimous   D. judgment   29.__

30.	A. procede	B. publicly	C. sincerity	D. successful	30.____
31.	A. deceive	B. goverment	C. preferable	D. repetitive	31.____
32.	A. emphasis	B. skillful	C. advisible	D. optimistic	32.____
33.	A. tendency	B. rescind	C. crucial	D. noticable	33.____
34.	A. privelege	B. abbreviate	C. simplify	D. divisible	34.____

Questions 35-43.

DIRECTIONS: Each of Questions 35 to 43 consists of four names. For each question, select the one of the four names that should be FOURTH if the four names were arranged in alphabetical order in accordance with the Rules for Alphabetical Filing given below. Read these rules carefully. Then, for each question, indicate in the correspondingly numbered space at the right the letter preceding the name that should be FOURTH in alphabetical order.

RULES FOR ALPHABETICAL FILING

NAMES OF INDIVIDUALS

(1)   File all names of individuals in strict alphabetical order, first according to the last name, then according to first name or initial, and finally according to middle name or initial. For example: George Brown precedes Edward Hunt, and Charles N. Smith precedes David A. Smith.

(2)   Where the last names are identical, the one with an initial instead of a first name precedes the one with a first name beginning with the same initial. For example: G. Brown and G.B. Brown precede George A. Brown.

(3)   Where two identical last names also have identical first names or initials, the one without a middle name or initial precedes the one with a middle name or initial. For example: William Jones precedes both William B. Jones and William Bruce Jones.

(4)   When two last names are identical and the two first names or initials are also identical, the one with a middle initial precedes the one with a middle name beginning with the same initial. For example: William B. Jones precedes William Bruce Jones.

(5)   Prefixes such as D', De, La, and Le are considered parts of the names they precede. For example: George De Gregory precedes Arthur Dempsey.

(6)   Last names beginning with "Mac" or "Mc" are to be filed as spelled.

(7)   Abbreviated names are to be treated as if they were spelled out. For example: Chas. is filed as Charles, and Wm. is filed as William.

(8)   Titles and designations such as Dr., Mr., and Prof, are to be disregarded in filing.

NAMES OF BUSINESS ORGANIZATIONS

(1)   File names of business organizations exactly as written, except that an organization bearing the name of an individual is filed alphabetically according to the name of the individual in accordance with the rules for filing names of individuals given above. For example: Samuel Eartnett Lumber Company precedes Mutual Grocery Company.

(2)   Where numerals occur in a name, they are to be treated as if they were spelled out. For example: 5 stands for five and 9th stands for ninth.

(3)   Where the following words occur in names, they are to be disregarded: the, of, and.

SAMPLE:
    A. William Brown   (2)
    B. Arthur F. Browne   (4)
    C. Arthur Browne   (3)
    D. F. Brown   (1)

The numbers in parentheses indicate the proper alphabetical order in which these names should be filed. Since the name that should be filed FOURTH is Arthur F. Browne, the answer is B.

35. A. Francis Lattimore   B. H. Latham   35._
    C. G. Lattimore   D. Hugh Latham

36. A. Thomas B. Morgan   B. Thomas Morgan   36._
    C. T. Morgan   D. Thomas Bertram Morgan

37. A. Lawrence A. Villon   B. Chas. Valente   37._
    C. Charles M. Valent   D. Lawrence De Villon

38. A. Alfred Devance   B. A.R. D'Amico   38._
    C. Arnold De Vincent   D. A. De Pino

39. A. Dr. Milton A. Bergmann   B. Miss Evelyn M. Bergmenn   39._
    C. Prof. E.N. Bergmenn   D. Mrs. L.B. Bergmann

40. A. George MacDougald   B. Thomas McHern   40._
    C. William Macholt   D. Frank McHenry

41. A. Third National Bank   B. Robt. Tempkin Corp.   41._
    C. 32nd Street Carpet Co.   D. Wm. Templeton, Inc.

42. A. Mary Lobell Art Shop   B. John La Marca, Inc.   42._
    C. Lawyers' Guild   D. Frank Le Goff Studios

43. A. 9th Avenue Garage   B. Jos. Nuren Food Co.   43._
    C. The New Book Store   D. Novelty Card Corp.

Questions 44-50.

DIRECTIONS: Questions 44 to 50 are to be answered on the basis of the following Code Table. In this table, for each number a corresponding code letter is given. Each of the questions contains three pairs of numbers and code letters. In each pair, the code letters should correspond with the numbers in accordance with the Code Table.

<u>CODE TABLE</u>

Number	1	2	3	4	5	6	7	8	9	0
Corresponding Code Letter	Y	N	Z	X	W	T	U	P	S	R

In some of the pairs below, an error exists in the coding. Examine the pairs in each question carefully.
If an error exists in:
   only one of the pairs in the question, mark your answer A
   any two pairs in the question, mark your answer B all three pairs in the question, mark your answer C none of the pairs in the question, mark your answer D

SAMPLE:
       37258   -   ZUNWP
       948764 -   SXPTTX
       73196   -   UZYSP

In the above sample, the first pair is correct since each number, as listed, has the correct corresponding code letter. In the second pair, an error exists because the number 7 should have the code letter U instead of the letter T. In the third pair, an error exists because the number 6 should have the code letter T instead of the letter P. Since there are errors in two of the three pairs, the correct answer is B.

44.   493785 - XSZUPW   44._____
      86398207 - PTUSPNRU
      5943162 - WSXZYTN

45.   5413968412 - WXYZSTPXYR   45._____
      8763451297 - PUTZXWYZSU
      4781965302 - XUPYSUWZRN

46.   79137584 - USYRUWPX   46._____
      638247 - TZPNXS
      49679312 - XSTUSZYN

47.   37854296 - ZUPWXNST   47._____
      09183298 - RSYXZNSP
      91762358 - SYUTNXWP

48.   3918762485 - ZSYPUTNXPW   48._____
      1578291436 - YWUPNSYXZT
      2791385674 - NUSYZPWTUX

49. 197546821 - YSUWSTPNY
     873024867 - PUZRNWPTU
     583179246 - WPZYURNXT

49. ___

50. 510782463 - WYRUSNXTZ
     478192356 - XUPYSNZWT
     961728532 - STYUNPWXN

50. ___

KEY (CORRECT ANSWERS)

1.	C	11.	D	21.	A	31.	B	41.	C
2.	A	12.	A	22.	D	32.	C	42.	A
3.	B	13.	B	23.	D	33.	D	43.	B
4.	D	14.	A	24.	B	34.	A	44.	A
5.	C	15.	C	25.	B	35.	C	45.	C
6.	B	16.	D	26.	D	36.	D	46.	B
7.	A	17.	A	27.	A	37.	A	47.	B
8.	B	18.	C	28.	C	38.	C	48.	D
9.	D	19.	B	29.	B	39.	B	49.	C
10.	A	20.	A	30.	A	40.	B	50.	B

EXAMINATION SECTION
TEST 1

DIRECTIONS: Each question or incomplete statement is followed by several suggested answers or completions. Select the one that BEST answers the question or completes the statement. *PRINT THE LETTER OF THE CORRECT ANSWER IN THE SPACE AT THE RIGHT.*

1. A city employee should realize that in his contacts with the public,　　　　　1.____

    A. he should always agree with what a visitor says because *the customer is always right*
    B. he should not give any information over the telephone unless the caller identifies himself
    C. the manner in which he treats a visitor may determine the visitor's opinion of government employees generally
    D. visitors should at all times be furnished with all the information they request

2. The one of the following that is LEAST useful to a clerk employed in the mail unit of a large city department is knowing the　　　　　2.____

    A. functions of the various divisions in the department
    B. names of the various division heads
    C. location of the various divisions
    D. salaries of the various division heads

3. A clerk notices that a visitor has just entered the office. The other clerks are not aware of the visitor's presence. The MOST appropriate of the following actions for the clerk to take is to　　　　　3.____

    A. attend to the visitor immediately
    B. continue with his own work and leave the handling of the visitor to one of the other clerks
    C. cough loudly to direct the attention of the other clerks to the presence of the visitor
    D. continue with his work unless the visitor addresses him directly

4. When a record is borrowed from the files, the file clerk puts a substitution or *out* card in its place.
Of the following, the information that is LEAST commonly placed on the *out* card is　　　　　4.____

    A. who borrowed the record
    B. when the record was borrowed
    C. why the record was borrowed
    D. what record was borrowed

5. Of the following, the BEST method of maintaining a mailing list that is subject to frequent changes is to keep the names in a　　　　　5.____

    A. loose-leaf address book in which twenty names are entered on each page
    B. card file in which each name is entered on a separate card
    C. bound address book in which twenty-five names are entered on each page
    D. card file in which ten names are entered on each card

6. Of the following, the MAIN reason for using window envelopes instead of plain envelopes in mailing correspondence is that   6._____

    A. window envelopes cost less
    B. the address is less likely to be defaced during delivery
    C. addressing the envelopes is eliminated
    D. the postal rate for window envelopes is less

7. It is frequently helpful to file material under two subjects. In such a case, the material is filed under one subject and a card indicating where the material is filed is placed under the other subject.
This card is known GENERALLY as a _____ card.   7._____

    A. follow-up or tickler   B. guide
    C. transfer   D. cross-reference

8. In taking down a telephone message for an employee who is absent from the office, a clerk should consider it LEAST important to indicate in his note to the absent employee the   8._____

    A. time the call was received
    B. number of the telephone extension on which the call came in
    C. name of the clerk who took the message
    D. caller's telephone number

9. A mail clerk whose supervisor has instructed him to send certain items by *parcel post* should send them by   9._____

    A. fourth-class mail   B. Railway Express
    C. registered first class mail   D. second-class mail

10. Of the following, the MOST appropriate greeting for a receptionist to use in addressing visitors is   10._____

    A. "Please state your business."
    B. "May I help you?"
    C. "Hello. What is your problem?"
    D. "Do you wish to see someone?"

11. A clerk assigned to the task of adding several long columns of figures performs this work on an adding machine that prints the figures on a paper tape.
In general, the MOST efficient of the following methods of checking the accuracy of the computations is for the clerk to   11._____

    A. check the figures on the paper tape against the corresponding figures in the original material
    B. repeat the computations on the adding machine, using the figures appearing on the paper tape, and then check to see whether the totals on the two tapes are the same
    C. perform the computations manually and check the totals thus obtained against the totals obtained by machine operation
    D. have another clerk repeat the computations manually and check the totals obtained in these two sets of computations

12. The term *via* means MOST NEARLY   12.____

    A. by way of   B. face to face
    C. return postage guaranteed   D. value indicated above

13. A clerk assigned to open and sort incoming mail notices that an envelope does not con-   13.____
    tain the enclosure referred to in the letter.
    The MOST appropriate of the following actions for him to take is to

    A. delay the delivery of the letter for one day since the enclosure may turn up in the
        next day's mail
    B. forward the letter to the person to whom it is addressed with an indication that the
        enclosure was omitted
    C. forward the letter to the person to whom it is addressed and send a tracer inquiry to
        the post office
    D. return the letter to the writer with a request for the enclosure mentioned in the letter

14. To obtain MOST quickly the telephone number of the General Post Office in the tele-   14.____
    phone directory, one should look FIRST under the listing

    A. General Post Office   B. Federal Government
    C. United States Government   D. Post Office Department

15. While your supervisor is at lunch, a visitor approaches you and asks for information   15.____
    regarding an important matter. Although you have no information about the matter, you
    know that your supervisor has just received a confidential report on the subject and that
    the report is still in your supervisor's desk.
    The MOST appropriate of the following actions for you to take is to

    A. obtain the report from your supervisor's desk and permit the visitor to read it in
        your presence
    B. tell the visitor that your supervisor has just received a report on this matter and
        suggest that the visitor ask your supervisor for permission to read it
    C. inform the visitor that you have no information on the matter and suggest that he
        return later when the supervisor will be back from lunch
    D. obtain the report from your supervisor's desk and answer the visitor's questions
        from information contained in the report

16. The two sets of initials that are usually placed on the bottom of a business letter flush   16.____
    with the left-hand margin and on a line with the last line of the signature indicate

    A. where the letter should be filed
    B. who dictated the letter and who typed it
    C. which persons received copies of the letter
    D. how the letter should be routed

17. When payment of the personal check of a depositor is guaranteed by his bank, that   17.____
    check is called a

    A. bank draft   B. voucher check
    C. cashier's check   D. certified check

18. The *Ditto* machine is a(n) _____ machine.   18.____

    A. duplicating   B. transcribing
    C. dictating   D. adding

19. The classified telephone directory is known GENERALLY as The   19.____

    A. Consumers' Buying Guide   B. Business Index
    C. Red Book   D. Commodity Exchange

20. Department X employs 500 men who work in 20 different skilled trades. These men are   20.____
paid at an hourly rate which differs for each skilled trade. They are paid weekly. The number of hours worked by a man varies from week to week. The timekeeping clerk com-
putes the number of hours a week worked by each man, and the following devices that
may be used each week to determine the weekly earnings of each of these 500 men, the
one that will be MOST helpful to the payroll clerk, is a

    A. listing type of adding machine
    B. non-listing type of adding machine
    C. graph showing the average number of hours worked and the average hourly rate of
        pay for each week of the previous year
    D. table listing the amounts obtained by multiplying hourly rates of pay by number of
        hours worked

21. A cash fund kept on hand for the payment of minor office expenses is known GENER-   21.____
ALLY as

    A. petty cash   B. a sinking fund
    C. a drawing account   D. net assets

22. The term that describes the connection between the inter-office computer technology is   22.____

    A. interface   B. network
    C. hardware   D. software

23. Complaints from the public are no longer regarded by government officials as mere nui-   23.____
sances. Instead, complaints are often welcomed because they frequently bring into the
open conditions and faults in operation and service which should be corrected.
This statement means MOST NEARLY that

    A. government officials now realize that complaints from the public are necessary
    B. faulty operations and services are not brought into the open except by complaints
        from the public
    C. government officials now realize that complaints from the public are in reality a sign
        of a well-run organization
    D. complaints from the public can be useful in indicating needs for improvement in
        operation and service

Questions 24-26.

DIRECTIONS: Questions 24 to 26 are to be answered SOLELY on the basis of the informa-
                 tion contained in the following statement.

*The most important unit of the mimeograph machine is a perforated metal drum over
which is stretched a cloth ink pad. A reservoir inside the drum contains the ink which flows
through the perforations and saturates the ink pad. To operate the machine, the operator first
removes from the machine the protective sheet, which keeps the ink from drying while the
machine is not in use. He then hooks the stencil face down on the drum, draws the stencil*

smoothly over the drum, and fastens the stencil at the bottom. The speed with which the drum turns determines the blackness of the copies printed. Slow turning gives heavy, black copies; fast turning gives light, clear-cut reproductions. If reproductions are run on other than porous paper, slip-sheeting is necessary to prevent smearing. Often the printed copy fails to drop readily as it comes from the machine. This may be due to static electricity. To remedy this difficulty, the operator fastens a strip of tinsel from side to side near the impression roller so that the printed copy just touches the soft stems of the tinsel as it is ejected from the machine, thus grounding the static electricity to the frame of the machine.

24. According to this statement,   24._____

    A.   turning the drum fast produces light copies
    B.   stencils should be placed face up on the drum
    C.   ink pads should be changed daily
    D.   slip-sheeting is necessary when porous paper is being used

25. According to this statement, when a mimeograph machine is not in use, the   25._____

    A.   ink should be drained from the drum
    B.   ink pad should be removed
    C.   machine should be covered with a protective sheet
    D.   counter should be set at zero

26. According to this statement, static electricity is grounded to the frame of the mimeograph   26._____
    machine by means of

    A.   a slip-sheeting device
    B.   a strip of tinsel
    C.   an impression roller
    D.   hooks located at the top of the drum

Questions 27-28.

DIRECTIONS: Questions 27 and 28 are to be answered SOLELY on the basis of the information contained in the following statement.

The proofreading of material typed from copy is performed more accurately and more speedily when two persons perform this work as a team. The person who did not do the typing should read aloud the original copy while the person who did the typing should check the reading against the typed copy. The reader should speak very slowly and repeat the figures, using a different grouping of numbers when repeating the figures. For example, in reading 1967, the reader may say 'one-nine-six-seven' on first reading the figure and 'nineteen-sixty-seven' on repeating the figure. The reader should read all punctuation marks, taking nothing for granted. Since mistakes can occur anywhere, everything typed should be proofread. To avoid confusion, the proofreading team should use the standard proofreading marks, which are given in most dictionaries.

27. According to this statement,

    A. the person who holds the typed copy is called the reader
    B. the two members of a proofreading team should take turns in reading the typed copy aloud
    C. the typed copy should be checked by the person who did the typing
    D. the person who did not do the typing should read aloud from the typed copy

27.____

28. According to this statement,

    A. it is unnecessary to read the period at the end of a sentence
    B. typographical errors should be noted on the original copy
    C. each person should develop his own set of proofreading marks
    D. figures should be read twice

28.____

29. When questioned by his supervisor, the clerk said, *"I have never begin a new assignment until I have completely finished whatever I am working on."*
This statement may BEST be characterized as

    A. *foolish;* work should be orderly
    B. *foolish;* every task must be completed sooner or later
    C. *wise;* unfinished work is an index of inefficiency
    D. *foolish;* some assignments should be undertaken immediately

29.____

30. Suppose that a clerk in your office has been transferred to another unit. After a brief period of training, you are assigned to his duties. An important problem arises, and you are uncertain as to the most advisable course of action.
For you to telephone the clerk whose place you are taking and to ask his advice would be

    A. *wise;* his interest in your welfare will be stimulated
    B. *foolish;* incompetence is admitted
    C. *foolish;* learning is best accomplished by doing
    D. *wise;* useful guidance may be obtained

30.____

31. Suppose that a file cabinet, which has a capacity of 3,000 cards, now contains approximately 2,200 cards. Cards are added to the file at the average rate of 30 cards a day.
To find the number of days it will take to fill the cabinet to capacity,

    A. divide 3,000 by 30
    B. divide 2,200 by 3,000
    C. divide 800 by 30
    D. multiply 30 by the fraction 2,200 divided by 3,000

31.____

32. A *tickler file* is used CHIEFLY for

    A. unsorted papers which the file clerk has not had time to file
    B. personnel records
    C. pending matters which should receive attention at some particular time
    D. index to cross-referenced material

32.____

33. A new file clerk who has not become thoroughly familiar with the files in unable to locate   33.____
    McLeod in the correspondence files under *Mo* and asks your help.
    Of the following, the BEST reply to give her is that

    A. there probably is no correspondence in the files for that person
    B. she probably has the name spelled wrong and should verify the spelling
    C. she will probably find the correspondence under *McLeod* as the files are arranged
       with the prefix *Mc* considered as *Mac* (as if the name were spelled *MacLeod*)
    D. the correspondence folder for *McLeod* has evidently been misplaced or borrowed
       from the files

34. If your superior asks you a question to which you do not know the answer, you should   34.____
    say

    A. "That is not my work."
    B. "I'm sorry, I do not know."
    C. "I do not know but you can look it up in the files."
    D. "Ask Miss Jones. I think she knows something about that matter."

35. Of the following, for which reason are cross-references necessary in filing?   35.____

    A. There is a choice of terms under which the correspondence may be filed.
    B. The only filing information contained in the correspondence is the name of the
       writer.
    C. Records are immediately visible without searching through the files.
    D. Persons other than file clerks can easily locate material.

36. The Federal Bureau of Investigation is a bureau in the Department of   36.____

    A. Justice   B. Defense   C. the Interior   D. State

37. A citizen of the United States who wishes to obtain a passport permitting him to visit a   37.____
    foreign country should apply at the office of the United States Department of

    A. Defense   B. Justice   C. the Interior   D. State

38. The permanent headquarters of the United Nations is in   38.____

    A. Geneva   B. Moscow   C. Paris   D. New York City

39. Six gross of special drawing pencils were purchased for use in a city department.   39.____
    If the pencils were used at the rate of 24 a week, the MAXIMUM number of weeks that
    the six gross of pencils would last is _____ weeks.

    A. 6   B. 12   C. 24   D. 36

40. A stock clerk had 600 pads on hand. He then issued 3/8 of his supply of pads to Division   40.____
    X, 1/4 to Division Y, and 1/6 to Division Z.
    The number of pads remaining in stock is

    A. 48   B. 125   C. 240   D. 475

41. If a certain job can be performed by 18 clerks in 26 days, the number of clerks needed to   41.____
    perform the job in 12 days is _____ clerks.

    A. 24   B. 30   C. 39   D. 52

Questions 42-50.

DIRECTIONS: Each of Questions 42 to 50 consists of four names. For each question, select the one of the four names that should be THIRD if the four names were arranged in alphabetical order in accordance with the Rules for Alphabetical Filing given below. For each question, print in the correspondingly numbered space at the right the letter preceding the name that should be THIRD in alphabetical order.

RULES FOR ALPHABETICAL FILING

NAMES OF INDIVIDUALS

(1)   Names of individuals are to be filed in strict alphabetical order. This order is determined first according to the last name, then according to the first name or initial, and finally according to the middle name or initial (if any).

(2)   Where two last names are identical, the one with an initial instead of a first name precedes the one with a first name that begins with the same initial letter. For example: Cole precedes Edward Cole.

(3)   Where two last names are identical and the two first names are also identical, the one without a middle name or initial precedes the one with a middle name or initial. For example: Edward Cole precedes both Edward R. Cole and Edward Robert Cole.

(4)   Where two last names are identical and the two first names are also identical, the one with a middle initial precedes the one with a middle name beginning with the same initial letter.
For example: Edward R. Cole precedes Edward Robert Cole.

(5)   Prefixes such as D', De, La, Le, Mac, Mc, O', and von are considered parts of the names they precede. These names should be filed as spelled. For example: Peter La Farge precedes John Le Blanc.

(6)   Treat all abbreviations as if spelled out in full when the names for which they stand are commonly understood.

NAMES OF BUSINESS ORGANIZATIONS

(1)   Names of business organizations are filed in alphabetical order as written, except that a name containing the name of an individual is filed in accordance with the rules given for filing names of individuals. For example: John Cole Varnish Co. precedes Federal Trust Co.

(2)   Names composed of numerals or abbreviations are to be treated as though the numerals or abbreviations were spelled out.

(3)   Disregard the following in alphabetizing: and, the, of.

SAMPLE:

    (A) Adam Dunn   (2)
    (B) E. Dunn   (3)
    (C) A. Duncan   (1)
    (D) Edward Robert Dunn (4)

The numbers in parentheses indicate the proper alphabetical order in which these names should be filed. Since the name that should be filed THIRD is E. Dunn, the answer is B.

42. A. William Carver   B. Howard Cambell   42._____
     C. Arthur Chambers   D. Charles Banner

43. A. Paul Moore   B. William Moore   43._____
     C. Paul A. Moore   D. William Allen Moore

44. A. George Peters   B. Eric Petersen   44._____
     C. G. Peters   D. Petersen

45. A. Edward Hallam   B. Jos. Frank Hamilton 45._____
     C. Edward A. Hallam   D. Joseph F. Hamilton

46. A. Theodore Madison   B. Timothy McGill   46._____
     C. Thomas MacLane   D. Thomas A. Madison

47. A. William O'Hara   B. Arthur Gordon   47._____
     C. James DeGraff   D. Anne von Glatin

48. A. Charles Green   B. Chas. T. Greene   48._____
     C. Charles Thomas Greene D. Wm. A. Greene

49. A. John Foss Insurance Co. B. New World Stove Co. 49._____
     C. 14th Street Dress Shop D. Arthur Stein Paper Co.

50. A. Gold Trucking Co.   B. 8th Ave. Garage   50._____
     C. The First National Bank D. The Century Novelty Co.

KEY (CORRECT ANSWERS)

1. C	11. A	21. A	31. C	41. C
2. D	12. A	22. B	32. C	42. A
3. A	13. B	23. D	33. C	43. B
4. C	14. C	24. A	34. B	44. D
5. B	15. C	25. C	35. A	45. D
6. C	16. B	26. B	36. A	46. D
7. D	17. D	27. C	37. D	47. A
8. B	18. A	28. D	38. D	48. C
9. A	19. C	29. C	39. D	49. B
10. B	20. D	30. C	40. B	50. C

—————

TEST 2

DIRECTIONS: Each question or incomplete statement is followed by several suggested answers or completions. Select the one that BEST answers the question or completes the statement. *PRINT THE LETTER OF THE CORRECT ANSWER IN THE SPACE AT THE RIGHT.*

1. *The supervisor's instructions were terse.* The word *terse* as used in this sentence means MOST NEARLY

    A. detailed   B. harsh   C. vague   D. concise

1.____

2. *He did not wish to evade these issues.* The word *evade* as used in this sentence means MOST NEARLY

    A. avoid   B. examine   C. settle   D. discuss

2.____

3. *The prospects for an early settlement were dubious.* The word *dubious* as used in this sentence means MOST NEARLY

    A. strengthened   B. uncertain   C. weakened   D. cheerful

3.____

4. *The visitor was morose.* The word *morose* as used in this sentence means MOST NEARLY

    A. curious   B. gloomy   C. impatient   D. timid

4.____

5. *He was unwilling to impede the work of his unit.* The word *impede* as used in this sentence means MOST NEARLY

    A. carry out   B. criticize   C. praise   D. hinder

5.____

6. *The remuneration was unsatisfactory.* The word *remuneration* as used in this sentence means MOST NEARLY

    A. payment   B. summary   C. explanation   D. estimate

6.____

7. A *recurring* problem is one that

    A. replaces a problem that existed previously
    B. is unexpected
    C. has long been overlooked
    D. comes up from time to time

7.____

8. *His subordinates were aware of this magnanimous act.* The word *magnanimous* as used in this sentence means MOST NEARLY

    A. insolent   B. shrewd   C. unselfish   D. threatening

8.____

9. *The new employee is a zealous worker.* The word *zealous* as used in this sentence means MOST NEARLY

    A. awkward   B. untrustworthy
    C. enthusiastic   D. skillful

9.____

10. To *impair* means MOST NEARLY to

    A. weaken   B. conceal   C. improve   D. expose

10.____

11. *The unit head was in a quandary.* The word *quandary* as used in this sentence means   11.____
    MOST NEARLY

    A. violent dispute   B. puzzling predicament
    C. angry mood   D. strong position

12. *His actions were judicious.* The word *judicious* as used in this sentence means MOST   12.____
    NEARLY

    A. wise   B. biased   C. final   D. limited

13. *His report contained many irrelevant statements.* The word *irrelevant* as used in this sen-   13.____
    tence means MOST NEARLY

    A. unproven   B. not pertinent
    C. hard to understand   D. insincere

14. *He was not present at the inception of the program.* The word *inception* as used in this   14.____
    sentence means MOST NEARLY

    A. beginning   B. discussion   C. conclusion   D. rejection

15. The word *solicitude* means MOST NEARLY   15.____

    A. request   B. isolation   C. seriousness   D. concern

Questions 16-30.

DIRECTIONS: Each of the sentences numbered 16 to 30 may be classified MOST appropri-
              ately under one of the following four categories:
              A. faulty because of incorrect grammar or word usage
              B. faulty because of incorrect punctuation
              C. faulty because of incorrect capitalization
              D. correct

              Examine each sentence carefully. Then, in the correspondingly numbered
              space at the right, print the letter preceding the option which is the BEST of the
              four suggested above. All incorrect sentences contain but one type of error.
              Consider a sentence correct if it contains none of the types of errors men-
              tioned, even though there may be other correct ways of expressing the same
              thought.

16. He was not informed, that he would have to work overtime.   16.____

17. The wind blew several papers off of his desk.   17.____

18. Charles Dole, who is a member of the committee, was asked to confer with commis-   18.____
    sioner Wilson.

19. Miss Bell will issue a copy to whomever asks for one.   19.____

20. Most employees, and he is no exception do not like to work overtime.   20.____

21. This is the man whom you interviewed last week.   21.____

22. Of the two cities visited, White Plains is the cleanest.   22.____

23. Although he was willing to work on other holidays, he refused to work on Labor day.   23.____

24. If an employee wishes to attend the conference, he should fill out the necessary forms.   24.____

25. The division chief reports that an engineer and an inspector is needed for this special survey.   25.____

26. The work was assigned to Miss Green and me.   26.____

27. The staff regulations state that an employee, who is frequently tardy, may receive a negative evaluation.   27.____

28. He is the kind of person who is always willing to undertake difficult assignments.   28.____

29. Mr. Wright's request cannot be granted under no conditions.   29.____

30. George Colt a new employee, was asked to deliver the report to the Domestic Relations Court.   30.____

Questions 31-40.

DIRECTIONS: Each of Questions 31 to 40 consists of four words. One of the words in each question is spelled INCORRECTLY. For each question, print in the correspondingly numbered space at the right the letter preceding the word which is INCORRECTLY spelled.

	A.		B.		C.		D.		
31.	A.	primery	B.	mechanic	C.	referred	D.	admissible	31.____
32.	A.	cessation	B.	beleif	C.	aggressive	D.	allowance	32.____
33.	A.	leisure	B.	authentic	C.	familiar	D.	contemptable	33.____
34.	A.	volume	B.	forty	C.	dilemma	D.	seldum	34.____
35.	A.	discrepancy	B.	aquisition	C.	exorbitant	D.	lenient	35.____
36.	A.	simultanous	B.	penetrate	C.	revision	D.	conspicuous	36.____
37.	A.	ilegible	B.	gracious	C.	profitable	D.	obedience	37.____
38.	A.	manufacturer	B.	authorize	C.	compelling	D.	pecular	38.____
39.	A.	anxious	B.	rehearsal	C.	handicaped	D.	tendency	39.____
40.	A.	meticulous	B.	accompaning	C.	initiative	D.	shelves	40.____

Questions 41-50.

DIRECTIONS: Questions 41 to 50 are based on the Personnel Record of Division X shown below. Refer to this table when answering these questions.

DIVISION X
PERSONNEL RECORD - CURRENT YEAR

Employee	Bureau in Which Employed	Title	Annual Salary	No. of Days Absent		No. of Times Late
				On Vaca-tion	On Sick Leave	
Abbott	Mail Bureau	Clerk	$31,200	18	0	1
Barnes	,,	Clerk	25,200	25	3	7
Davis	,,	Typist	24,000	21	9	2
Adams	Payroll Bureau	Accountant	42,500	10	0	2
Bell	,,	Bookkeeper	31,200	23	2	5
Duke	,,	Clerk	27,600	24	4	3
Gross	,,	Clerk	21,600	12	5	7
Lane	,,	Stenographer	26,400	19	16	20
Reed	,,	Typist	22,800	15	11	11
Arnold	Record Bureau	Clerk	32,400	6	15	9
Cane	,,	Clerk	24,500	14	3	4
Fay	,,	Clerk	21,100	20	0	4
Hale	,,	Typist	25,200	18	2	7
Baker	Supply Bureau	Clerk	30,000	20	3	2
Clark	,,	Clerk	27,600	25	6	5
Ford	,,	Typist	22,800	25	4	22

41.   The percentage of the total number of employees who are clerks is MOST NEARLY   41.___

   A.   25%   B.   33%   C.   38%   D.   56%

42.   Of the following employees, the one who receives a monthly salary of $2,100 is   42.___

   A.   Barnes   B.   Gross   C.   Reed   D.   Clark

43.   The difference between the annual salary of the highest paid clerk and that of the lowest   43.___
paid clerk is

   A. $6,000   B. $8,400   C. $11,300   D. $20,900

44.   The number of employees receiving more than $25,000 a year but less than $40,000 a   44.___
year is

   A.   6   B.   9   C.   12   D.   15

45.   The total annual salary of the employees of the Mail Bureau is   45.___

   A.   one-half of the total annual salary of the employees of the Payroll Bureau
   B.   less than the total annual salary of the employees of the Record Bureau by
       $21,600
   C.   equal to the total annual salary of the employees of the Supply Bureau
   D.   less than the total annual salary of the employees of the Payroll Bureau by $71,600

46.   The average annual salary of the employees who are NOT clerks is MOST NEARLY   46.___

   A. $23,700   B. $25,450   C. $26,800   D. $27,850

47. If all the employees were given a 10% increase in pay, the annual salary of Lane would then be   47.____

    A. greater than that of Barnes by $1,320
    B. less than that of Bell by $4,280
    C. equal to that of Clark
    D. greater than that of Ford by $3,600

48. Of the clerks who earned less than $30,000 a year, the one who was late the FEWEST   48.____
number of times was late _____ time(s).

    A. 1   B. 2   C. 3   D. 4

49. The bureau in which the employees were late the FEWEST number of times on an aver-   49.____
age is the _____ Bureau.

    A. Mail   B. Payroll   C. Record   D. Supply

50. The MOST accurate of the following statements is that   50.____

    A. Reed was late more often than any other typist
    B. Bell took more time off for vacation than any other employee earning $30,000 or more annually
    C. of the typists, Ford was the one who was absent the fewest number of times because of sickness
    D. three clerks took no time off because of sickness

_____

KEY (CORRECT ANSWERS)

1.	D	11.	B	21.	D	31.	A	41.	D
2.	A	12.	A	22.	A	32.	B	42.	A
3.	B	13.	B	23.	C	33.	D	43.	C
4.	B	14.	A	24.	D	34.	D	44.	B
5.	D	15.	D	25.	A	35.	B	45.	C
6.	A	16.	B	26.	D	36.	A	46.	D
7.	D	17.	A	27.	B	37.	A	47.	A
8.	C	18.	C	28.	D	38.	D	48.	C
9.	C	19.	A	29.	A	39.	C	49.	A
10.	A	20.	B	30.	B	40.	B	50.	B

_____

EXAMINATION SECTION
TEST 1

DIRECTIONS: Each question or incomplete statement is followed by several suggested answers or completions. Select the one that BEST answers the question or completes the statement. *PRINT THE LETTER OF THE CORRECT ANSWER IN THE SPACE AT THE RIGHT.*

1. Assume that you are one of several clerks employed in the office of a city department. Members of the public occasionally visit the office to obtain information. Because your desk is nearest the entrance to the office, most of these visitors direct their inquiries to you. One morning when every one including yourself is busy, a visitor enters the office and asks you for some readily available information.
   Of the following, the BEST action for you to take is to

   A. disregard his question in the hope that he will direct his inquiry to another clerk
   B. inform him politely that you are busy now and ask him to return in the afternoon
   C. give him the requested information concisely but courteously and then continue with your work
   D. advise him to write a letter to your department so that the information can be sent to him

1._____

2. As a clerk in the payroll bureau of a city department, you have been assigned the task of checking several payroll sheets. Your supervisor has informed you that these payroll sheets are needed by another department and must be sent to that department by 4 P.M. that day. After you have worked for a few hours, you realize that you will be unable to complete this assignment on time.
   Of the following, the BEST action for you to take first is to

   A. ask a co-worker to help you
   B. check only those payroll sheets which you think are most important
   C. make sure that the payroll sheets which have been checked are sent out on time
   D. inform your supervisor of the situation

2._____

3. The switchboard operator of Department X refers a call to the department's Personnel Bureau. Miss Jones, a clerk in the Personnel Bureau, answers this call.
   Of the following ways of answering this call, the MOST acceptable one is for Miss Jones to say

   A. "Hello."
   B. "Personnel Bureau, Miss Jones speaking."
   C. "Miss Jones speaking. To whom do you wish to speak?!'
   D. "Hello. This is Miss Jones of Department X."

3._____

4. A clerk in the mailing division of a large city department should be acquainted with the functions of the other divisions of the department CHIEFLY because he will be

   A. able to answer questions asked by visitors regarding the department
   B. more conscientious in doing his work if he knows that other divisions of the department perform important functions
   C. in a better position to make suggestions for improving the work of the various divisions of the department
   D. able to determine the proper division to which mail is to be forwarded

4._____

5. The central filing unit of a certain city department keeps in its files records used by the   5.____
    various bureaus in connection with their daily work.
    It is desirable for the clerks in this filing unit to refile records as soon as possible after they
    have been returned by the different bureaus CHIEFLY because

    A. records which are needed can be located most easily if they have been filed
    B. such procedure develops commendable work habits among the employees
    C. records which are not filed immediately are usually filed incorrectly
    D. the accumulation of records to be filed gives the office a disorderly appearance

6. The active and inactive file material of an office is to be filed in several four-drawer filing   6.____
    cabinets.
    Of the following, the BEST method of filing the material is, in general, to

    A. keep inactive material in the upper drawers of the file cabinet so that such material
        may be easily removed for disposal
    B. keep active material in the upper drawers so that the amount of stooping by clerks
        using the files is reduced to a minimum
    C. assign drawers in the file cabinets alternately to active and to inactive material so
        that file material can be transferred easily from the active to the inactive files
    D. assign file cabinets alternately to active and to inactive material so that
        cross-references between the two types of material can be easily made

7. Of the following, the BEST reason for using form letters is that they   7.____

    A. enable an individual to transmit unpleasant or disappointing communications in a
        gentle and sympathetic manner
    B. present the facts in a terse, business-like manner
    C. save the time of both the dictator and the typist in answering letters dealing with
        similar matters
    D. are flexible and can be easily changed to meet varying needs and complex
        situations

8. City agencies use either window envelopes or plain envelopes in mailing their   8.____
    correspondence, depending upon the type of mail being sent out.
    When a mail clerk uses a window envelope rather than a plain envelope, he should be
    especially careful in

    A. sealing and stamping the envelope
    B. affixing the correct amount of postage
    C. folding and inserting the communication
    D. checking the return address

9. As a mail clerk, you have been instructed to make sure that an important letter is received   9.____
    by the person to whom it is addressed.

    Of the following, the BEST action for you to take is to send the letter by
    A. registered mail   B. special delivery
    C. air mail   D. first-class mail

3

10. In filing, a clerk must often attach several papers together before placing them in the files. 10._____
    Usually, the MOST desirable of the following methods of attaching these papers is to

    A. pin them together
    B. staple them together
    C. attach them with a paper clip
    D. glue them together

11. It is a common practice in answering a letter of inquiry to make a copy of the reply. 11._____
    A clerk should know that, of the following, the BEST procedure to follow with the copy
    is to

    A. file it with the letter it answers
    B. file it alphabetically in a separate copy file
    C. file it chronologically in a separate copy file and destroy the copy after thirty days
    D. enclose it with the letter of reply

12. Suppose that much of the work of your office involves computation of statistical data. 12._____
    This computation is being done without the use of adding machines. You believe the
    work could be done more efficiently if adding machines were used.
    Of the following, the BEST action for you to take is to

    A. carry out your assignments without comment, since it is not your function to
       recommend revisions in office practices
    B. have other clerks who agree with you sign a memorandum requesting your
       supervisor to install adding machines
    C. obtain concrete facts to support your views and then take this matter up with
       your supervisor
    D. point out to your supervisor every time an error is made that it would not have
       occurred if adding machines had been used

13. A clerk employed in the central file section of a city department has been requested to 13._____
    obtain a certain card which is kept in an alphabetic file containing several thousand cards.
    The clerk finds that this card is not in its proper place and that there is no out card to aid
    him in tracing its location.
    Of the following, the course of action which would be LEAST helpful to him in locating the
    missing card would be for him to

    A. secure the assistance of his superior
    B. look at several cards filed immediately before and after the place where the
       missing card should be filed
    C. ask the other clerks in the file section whether they have this card
    D. prepare an out card and place it where the missing card should be filed

14. The one of the following types of computer software which requires the use of 14._____
    spreadsheets is

    A. Excel   B. Acrobat   C. Outlook   D. Safari

15. A clerk assigned to file correspondence in a subject file would be MOST concerned with 15._____
    the
    A. name of the sender   B. main topic of the correspondence
    C. city and state of the sender   D. date of the correspondence

55

16. Assume that you are responsible for storing and distributing supplies in a city department. 16.____
The one of the following factors which you should consider LEAST important in selecting a
suitable place in the stock room for storing a particular item is

    A. the frequency of requests for it
    B. its perishability
    C. its size
    D. the importance of the bureaus using it

17. A clerk in charge of the supply room of a city department notices that one of the bureaus 17.____
is asking for considerably more stationery than it has requested in the past.
For him to inquire into the reasons for the increased demand would be

    A. *desirable*; the amount of stationery used by a bureau should remain constant
    B. *undesirable*; the increased demand may be due to waste, a condition beyond his control
    C. *desirable*; he will be better able to estimate future needs for stationery
    D. *undesirable*; he may be accused of meddling in matters which do not concern him

18. One of the first things an executive usually looks for when he arrives in the morning is 18.____
his mail.
Of the following, the MOST valid implication on the basis of this statement is that

    A. letters addressed to an executive should be answered in the order in which
       they are received
    B. whenever possible, mail for an executive should be on his desk before his
       arrival in the morning
    C. letters to a city department should be addressed to the department head
    D. the first task of an executive upon his arrival in the morning should be to
       answer his mail

19. Persons in the employ of a public agency generally come into contact with many people 19.____
outside of working hours. In these contacts, the government employee represents to the
public the quality, competence, and stature of public employees as a group.
The one of the following statements which is the MOST valid implication of the above
observation is that

    A. the responsibilities of a public employee cease after office hours
    B. government employees who come into contact with the public during working hours
       should be more efficient than those who have no contact with the public
    C. a public employee, by his behavior during social activities, can raise the prestige of
       public employment
    D. employees of a private company have greater responsibilities during office hours
       than employees of a public agency

20. Filing, in a way, is a form of recording. 20.____

    The one of the following which BEST explains this statement is that
    A. no other records are required if a proper filing system is used
    B. important records should, as a rule, be kept in filing cabinets
    C. a good system of record keeping eliminates the necessity for a filing system
    D. filing a letter or document is, in effect, equivalent to making a record of its contents

21. In standardizing clerical tasks, one should attempt to eliminate the undesirable elements   21._____
and to retain the desirable ones.
Of the following, the MOST valid implication of the above statement is that

    A. a task containing undesirable elements cannot be standardized
    B. standardized clerical tasks should not contain any unnecessary steps
    C. interesting clerical tasks are easier to standardize than monotonous clerical tasks
    D. a clerical task cannot have both desirable and undesirable elements

22. The efficiency of office workers in affected by the quality of the services provided to   22._____
facilitate their work.
The one of the following statements which is the BEST illustration of the above judgment
is that

    A. a poorly run mail room will hamper the work of the office staff
    B. continual tardiness on the part of an office worker will be reflected in the
erformance of his work
    C. a system of promoting office workers through competitive examinations will
increase their efficiency
    D. the use of a time clock will improve the quality of the work performed

23. In elections held in various states, the provisions relating to veterans' preference have   23._____
been amended to conform with Federal practice.
In general, the MOST accurate statement regarding veterans' preference in civil service
open competitive examinations for original appointment is that

    A. disabled veterans passing an examination will be given 10 additional points and
non-disabled veterans passing an examination will be given 5 additional points
    B. disabled veterans passing an examination will be placed on top of the eligible list;
non-disabled veterans will be placed after them; and non-veterans will be placed
last on the list
    C. only disabled veterans will be given 5 additional points; no additional points will
be given to nondisabled veterans
    D. the granting of additional points to all disabled and non-disabled veterans will be
discontinued

24. Suppose that you are assigned to the information desk in your department. Your function   24._____
is to give information to members of the public who telephone or call in person. It is a busy
period of the year. There is a line of seventeen people waiting to speak to you. Because you
are constantly being interrupted by telephone calls for information, however, you are unable
to give any attention to the people waiting on line. The line is increasing in length.
Of the following, the BEST action for you to take is to

    A. explain courteously to the people on line that you will probably be unable to help
them
    B. advise the people at the end of the line that you will probably not reach them for
some time and suggest that they come back when you are less busy
    C. ask the switchboard operator to answer telephone requests for information herself
instead of putting the calls on your extension
    D. ask your supervisor to assign another clerk to answer telephone calls so that you
can give your full attention to the people on line

6

25. Suppose that you are acting as the receptionist in your department. A man comes up to   25.____
you, introduces himself as Mr. Smith, and says that he has an appointment with Mr. Brown,
one of the clerks in your department. You know that Mr. Brown has been called out of the
office for a few days on important business. Upon learning of Mr. Brown's absence,
Mr. Smith asks whether someone else can help him. For you to telephone Mr. Brown's office
and ask whether some other clerk there can help Mr. Smith would be WISE mainly because

    A. Mr. Smith's business is probably confidential
    B. another clerk has probably been assigned to do Mr. Brown's work in Mr. Brown's
       absence
    C. Mr. Brown may return unexpectedly
    D. it is uncertain whether Mr. Smith actually does have an appointment with Mr. Brown

26. One of your duties may be to deliver copies of administrative orders to administrators   26.____
in your department. It is not necessary for an administrator to sign
a receipt for his copy of an order. One of the administrators to whom you are requested to
deliver a copy of an order is not at his desk when you make your usual tour of the office.
Of the following, the BEST action for you to take is to

    A. keep this order until a later order is issued and then deliver both orders at the same time
    B. wait until you meet the administrator in the corridor and give him his copy in person
    C. leave a note on the administrator's desk requesting him to call
    D. leave the administrator's copy of the order on his desk

27. One of your duties may be to deliver inter-office mail to all of the offices in the   27.____
department in which you work.
Of the following, the BEST procedure for you to follow before you deliver the letters is,
in general, to arrange them on the basis of the

    A. offices to which the letters are to be delivered
    B. dates on which the letters were written
    C. specific persons by whom the letters were signed
    D. offices from which the letters come

28. The population census of the country is undertaken every ten years by the United States   28.____
Department of
    A. Labor   B. the Treasury   C. Commerce   D. the Interior

29. Of the following pairs of offices in the Federal government, the pair which is held by the   29.____
same individual is
    A. Secretary of Defense and Secretary of the Army
    B. Chairman of the Atomic Energy Commission and Chairman of the Tennessee
       Valley Authority
    C. Chief Justice of the United States Supreme Court and Attorney General
    D. Vice President of the United States and President of the Senate

30. A clerk who is familiar with the organization and activities of the United Nations should   30.____
know, of the following statements, the MOST accurate one is that
    A. the permanent headquarters of the United Nations is in Geneva, Switzerland
    B. devaluation of the currency of a member nation must be approved by the
       United Nations General Assembly
    C. there are five permanent members on the United Nations Security Council
    D. the Economic Cooperation Administration (ECA) is under the jurisdiction of the
       United Nations Secretary General

58

31. In anticipation of a seasonal increase in the amount of work to be performed by his division, a division chief prepared the following list of additional temporary employees needed by his division and the amount of time they would be employed:
    26 cashiers, each at $24,000 a year, for 2 months
    15 laborers, each at $85.00 a day, for 50 days
    6 clerks, each at $21,000 a year, for 3 months
    The total approximate cost for this additional personnel would be MOST NEARLY

    A. $200,000   B. $250,000   C. $500,000   D. $600,000

31._____

32. A calculating machine company offered to sell a city agency 4 calculating machines at a discount of 15% from the list price, and to allow the agency $85 for each of its two old machines. The list price of the new machines is $625 per machine.
    If the city agency accepts this offer, the amount of money it will have to provide for the purchase of these four machines is

    A. $1,785   B. $2,295   C. $1,955   D. $1,836

32._____

33. A stationery buyer was offered bond paper at the following price scale:
    $2.86 per ream for the first 1,000 reams
    $2.60 per ream for the next 4,000 reams
    $2.40 per ream for each additional ream beyond 5,000 reams
    If the buyer ordered 10,000 reams of paper, the average cost per ream, computed to the NEAREST cent, was

    A. $2.48   B. $2.53   C. $2.62   D. $2.72

33._____

34. A clerk has 5.70% of his salary deducted for his retirement pension.
    If this clerk's annual salary is $20,400, the monthly deduction for his retirement pension is

    A. $298.20   B. $357.90   C. $1,162.80   D. $96.90

34._____

35. In a certain bureau, two-thirds of the employees are clerks and the remainder is typists. If there are 90 clerks, then the number of typists in this bureau is

    A. 135   B. 45   C. 120   D. 30

35._____

Questions 36-45.

DIRECTIONS: Assume that the code tables shown below are used by a city department in classifying its employees. Questions 36 to 45 are to be answered on the basis of these tables. In accordance with these code tables, each employee in the department is assigned a code number consisting of ten digits arranged from left to right in the following order:
    I.   Division in which Employed
    II.   Title of Position
    III. Annual Salary
    IV.   Age
    V.   Number of Years Employed in Department

    Example: A clerk is 21 years old, has been employed in the department for three years, and is working in the Supply Division at a yearly salary of $25,000. His code number should be 90-115-13-02-2.

Questions 36-45.

DIRECTIONS: Assume that the code tables shown below are used by a city department in classifying its employees. Questions 36 to 45 are to be answered on the basis of these tables. In accordance with these code tables, each employee in the department is assigned a code number consisting of ten digits arranged from left to right in the following order:

VI.   Division in which Employed
VII. Title of Position
VIII. Annual Salary
IX.   Age
X.   Number of Years Employed in Department

Example: A clerk is 21 years old, has been employed in the department for three years, and is working in the Supply Division at a yearly salary of $25,000. His code number should be 90-115-13-02-2.

DEPARTMENTAL CODE

TABLE I		TABLE II		TABLE III		TABLE IV		TABLE V	
Code No.	Division in Which Employed	Code No.	Title of position	Code No.	Annual Salary	Code No.	Age	Code No.	No. of years Employed in Dept.
10-	Accounting Division	115-	Clek	11-	$18,000 or less	01-	under 20 yrs	1-	less than 1 yrs
20-	Construction Division	155-	Typist	12-	$18,001 to $24,000	02-	20 to 29 yrs	2-	1 to 5 yrs
30-	Engineering Division	175-	Steno-grapher	13-	$24,001 to $30,000	03-	30 to 39 yrs	3-	6 to 10 yrs
40-	Information Division	237-	Book-Keeper	14-	$30,001 to $36,000	04-	40 to 49 yrs	4-	11 to 15 yrs
50-	Maintenance Division	345-	Statis-tician	15-	$36,001 to $45,000	05-	50 to 59 yrs	5-	16 to 25 yrs
60-	Personnel Division	545-	Store-Keeper	16-	$45,001 to $60,000	06-	62 to 69 yrs	6-	26 to 35 yrs
70-	Record Division	633-	Drafts-Man	17-	$60,001 to $70,000	07- over	70 yrs or over	7-	36 yrs. or over
80-	Research Division	665-	Civil-Engineer	18-	$70,001 or over				
90-	Supply Division	865-	Machinist						
		915-	Porter						

36. A draftsman employed in the Engineering Division yearly salary of $34,800 is 36 years   36._____
old and has employed in the department for 9 years.
He should be coded

    A. 20-633-13-04-3   B. 50-665-14-04-4
    C. 30-865-13-03-4   D. 30-633-14-03-3

37. A porter employed in the Maintenance Division at a yearly salary of $28,800 is 52 years   37._____
old and has been employed in the department for 6 years.
He should be coded

    A. 50-915-12-03-3   B. 90-545-12-05-3
    C. 50-915-13-05-3   D. 90-545-13-03-3

38. Richard White, who has been employed in the department for 12 years, receives $50,000   38._____
a year as a civil engineer in the Construction Division. He is 38 years old.
He should be coded
    A. 20-665-16-03-4   B. 20-665-15-02-1
    C. 20-633-14-04-2   D. 20-865-15-02-5

39. An 18-year-old clerk appointed to the department six months ago is assigned to the   39._____
Record Division. His annual salary is $21,600.
He should be coded

    A. 70-115-11-01-1   B. 70-115-12-01-1
    C. 70-115-12-02-1   D. 70-155-12-01-1

40. An employee has been coded 40-155-12-03-3.   40._____
Of the following statements made regarding this employee, the MOST accurate one is
that he is

    A. a clerk who has been employed in the department for at least 6 years
    B. a typist who receives an annual salary which does not exceed $24,000
    C. under 30 years of age and has been employed in the department for at least
       11 years
    D. employed in the Supply Division at a salary which exceeds $18,000 per annum

41. Of the following statements regarding an employee who is coded 60-175-13-01-2, the   41._____
LEAST accurate statement is that this employee
    A. is a stenographer in the Personnel Division
    B. has been employed in the department for at least one year
    C. receives an annual salary which exceeds $24,000
    D. is more than 20 years of age

42. The following are the names of our employees of the department with their code numbers: 42._____

James Black, 80-345-15-03-4;
William White, 30-633-14-03-4;
Sam Green, 80-115-12-02-3;
John Jones, 10-237-13-04-5.

If a salary increase is to be given to the employees who have been employed in the department for 11 years or more and who earn less than $36,001 a year, the two of the above employees who will receive a salary increase are

- A. John Jones and William White
- B. James Black and Sam Green
- C. James Black and William White
- D. John Jones and Sam Green

43. Code number 50-865-14-02-6, which has been assigned to a machinist, contains an obvious inconsistency. This inconsistency involves the figures   43.____

     A. 50-865   B. 865-14   C. 14-02   D. 02-6

44. Ten employees were awarded merit prizes for outstanding service during the year. Their code numbers were: 44.____

80-345-14-04-4	40-155-12-02-2
40-155-12-04-4	10-115-12-02-2
10-115-13-03-2	80-115-13-02-2
80-175-13-05-5	10-115-13-02-3
10-115-12-04-3	30-633-14-04-4

Of these ten outstanding employees, the number who were clerks employed in the Accounting Division at a salary ranging from $24,001 to $30,000 per annum is

     A. 1   B. 2   C. 3   D. 4

45. The MOST accurate of the following statements regarding the ten outstanding employees listed in Question 44 above is that   45.____

- A. fewer than half of the employees were under 40 years of age
- B. there were fewer typists than stenographers
- C. four of the employees were employed in the department 11 years or more
- D. two of the employees in the Research Division receive annual salaries ranging from $30,001 to $36,000

Questions 46-55.

DIRECTIONS: Questions 46 to 55 consist of groups of names. For each group, three different filing arrangements of the names in the group are given. In only one of these arrangements are the names in correct filing order according to the alphabetic filing rules which are given below. For each group, select the one arrangement, lettered A, B, or C, which is CORRECT and indicate in the space at the right the letter which corresponds to the CORRECT arrangement of names.

RULES FOR ALPHABETIC FILING

NAMES OF INDIVIDUALS

(1) The names of individuals are to be filed in strict alphabetic order. The order of filing is: first according to the last name; then according to the first name or initial; and finally according to the middle name or initial.

(2) Where two last names are identical, the one with an initial instead of the first name precedes the one with a first name beginning with the same initial letter. For example: D. Smith and D.J. Smith precede Donald Smith.

(3) Where two individuals with identical last names also have identical first names or initials, the one without a middle name or initial precedes the one with a middle name or initial. For example: D. Smith precedes D.J. Smith, and Donald Smith precedes Donald J. Smith.

(4) Where two individuals with identical last names also have identical first names or initials, the one with an initial instead of the middle name precedes the one with a middle name beginning with the same initial letter. For example: Donald J. Smith precedes Donald Joseph Smith.

NAMES OF BUSINESS ORGANIZATIONS

The names of business organizations are to be filed in alphabetic order as written, except that the names of an organization containing the name of an individual is filed alphabetically according to the name of the individual as described in the above rules. For example: John Burke Wine Co. precedes Central Storage Corp.

ADDITIONAL RULES

(1) Names composed of numerals or of abbreviations of names are to be treated as if the numerals or the abbreviations were spelled out.
(2) Prefixes such as De, Di, O', Le, and La are considered as part of the names they precede.
(3) Names beginning with "Mc" and "Mac" are to be filed as spelled.
(4) The following titles and designations are to be disregarded in filing: Dr., Mr., Jr., Sr., D.D.S., and M.D.
(5) The following are to be disregarded when they occur in the names of business organizations: the, of, and.

SAMPLE ITEM:

ARRANGEMENT A	ARRANGEMENT B	ARRANGEMENT C
Robert Morse	R. Moss	R. T. Morse
Ralph Nixon	R. T. Morse	Robert Morse
R. T. Morse	Ralph Nixon	R. Moss
R. Moss	Robert Morse	Ralph Nixon

The CORRECT arrangement is C; the answer should, therefore, be C

46. ARRANGMENT A	ARRANGEMENT B	ARRANGEMENT C 46.____
R. B. Stevens	Aled T. Stevens	R.Stevens
Chas. Stevennson	R. B. Stevens	Robert Stevens, Sr.
Robert Stevensm, Sr.	Robert Stevens, Sr.	Alfred T. Steven s
Alfred T. Stevens	Chas. Stevenson	Chas. Stevenson

47. ARRANGEMENT A	ARRANGEMENT B	ARRANGEMENT C 47.____
Mr. A. T. Breen	John Brewington	Dr. Otis C. Breen
Dr. Otis C. Breen	Amelia K. Brewington	Mr. A. T. Breen
Amelia K Brewington	Dr. Otis C. Breen	John Brewington
John Brewington	Mr. A. T. Breen	Amelia K. Brewington

48. ARRANGEMENT A   ARRANGEMENT B   ARRANGEMENT C   48._____

ARRANGEMENT A	ARRANGEMENT B	ARRANGEMENT C
J. Murphy	John Murphy	J. Murphy
J. J. Murphy	John J. Murphy	John Murphy
John Murphy	J. Murphy	J. J. Murphy
John J. Murphy	J. J. Murphy	John J. Murphy

49. ARRANGEMENT A   ARRANGEMENT B   ARRANGEMENT C   49._____

ARRANGEMENT A	ARRANGEMENT B	ARRANGEMENT C
Anthoney Dibuono	Geo. T. Burns, Jr.	George Burns, Sr.
George Burns, Sr	George Burns, Sr.	George T. Burns, Jr.
Geo. T. Burns, Jr.	Anthony DiBuono	Alan J. Byrnes
Alan J. Byrnes	Alan J. Byrnes	Anthony DiBuono

50. ARRANGEMENT A   ARRANGEMENT B   ARRANGEMENT C   50._____

ARRANGEMENT A	ARRANGEMENT B	ARRANGEMENT C
James Macauley	James Macauley	Bernard J. Macmahon
Frank A. Mclowery	Francis Macloughry	Francis MacLaughry
Francis Maclaughry	Bernard J.Macmahon	Frank A. McLowery
Bernard J. MacMahon	Frank A. McLowery	James Macauley

51. ARRANGEMENT A   ARRANGEMENT B   ARRANGEMENT C   51._____

ARRANGEMENT A	ARRANGEMENT B	ARRANGEMENT C
A. J. DiBartolo, Sr.	J. A. Bartolo	Anthony J. Bartolo
A. P.DiBartolo	Anthony J. Bartolo	J. A. Bartolo
J. A. Bartolo	A. J. DiBartolo	A. J. DiBartolo, Sr
Anthony J. Bartolo	A. J. DiBartolo, Sr.	A. P. DiBartolo

52. ARRANGEMENT A   ARRANGEMENT B   ARRANGEMENT C   52._____

ARRANGEMENT A	ARRANGEMENT B	ARRANGEMENT C
Edward Holmes Corp.	Edward Holmes Corp.	Hillside Trust Corp.
Hillside Trust Corp.	Hillside Trust Corp.	Edward Holmes Corp
Standard Insurance Co.	The Industrial Surety Co.	The Industrial Surety Co.
The Industrial Surety Co	Standard Insurance Co.	Standard Insurance Co.

53. ARRANGEMENT A   ARRANGEMENT B   53._____

ARRANGEMENT A	ARRANGEMENT B
Cooperative Credit Co.	Chas, Cooke Chemical Corp.
Chas. Cooke Chemical Corp.	Cooperative Credit Co.
John Fuller Baking Co.	4th Avenue Express Co.
4th Avenue Express Co.	John Fuller Baking Co.

ARRANGEMENT C
4th Avenue Express Co.
John Fuller Baking Co.
Chas. Cooke Chemical Corp.
Cooperative Credit Co.

54. ARRANGEMENT A   ARRANGEMENT B   ARRANGEMENT C   54._____

ARRANGEMENT A	ARRANGEMENT B	ARRANGEMENT C
Mr. R. McDaniels	F. L. Ramsey	Robert darling, Jr.
Robert Darling, Jr.	Mr. R. McDaniels	Charles DeRhone
F. L. Ramsey	Charles DeRhone	Mr. R. Mcdaniels
Charles DeRhone	Robert Darling, Jr.	F. L. Ramsey

64

55.

ARRANGEMENT A	ARRANGEMENT B	ARRANGEMENT C	55._____
New York Ominibus Corp.	John J. O'Brien Co.	Nova Scotia Canning Co.	
New York Shipping Co.	New York Ominibus Ciorp.	John J. O'Brien Co.	
Nove Scotia Canning Co.	New York Shipping Co.	New York Ominibus Corp.	
John J. O'Brien Co.	Nove Scotia Canning Co.	New York shipping Co.	

56. He was asked to *pacify* the visitor. The word pacify means MOST NEARLY   56._____

    A. escort   B. interview   C. calm   D. detain

57. To say that a certain document is *authentic* means MOST NEARLY that it is   57._____

    A. fictitious   B. well written   C. priceless   D. genuine

58. A clerk who is *meticulous* in performing his work is one who is   58._____

    A. alert to improved techniques
    B. likely to be erratic and unpredictable
    C. excessively careful of small details
    D. slovenly and inaccurate

59 A pamphlet which is *replete* with charts and graphs is one which   59._____

    A. deals with the construction of charts and graphs
    B. is full of charts and graphs
    C. substitutes illustrations for tabulated data
    D. is in need of charts and graphs

60. His former secretary was *diligent* in carrying out her duties. The word diligent means   60._____
MOST NEARLY

    A. incompetent   B. cheerful   C. careless   D. industrious

61. To supepsede means MOST NEARLY to   61._____

    A. take the place of   B. come before
    C. be in charge of   D. divide into equal parts

62. He sent the *irate* employee to the pepsonnel manager. The word *irate* means   62._____
MOST NEARLY

    A. irresponsible   B. untidy   C. insubordinate   D. angry

63. An *ambiguous* statement is one which is   63._____
    A forceful and convincing
    B capable of being understood in more than one sense
    C based upon good judgment and sound reasoning processes
    D uninteresting and too lengthy

64. To *extol* means MOST NEARLY to   64._____

    A. summon   B. praise   C. reject   D. withdraw

65. The word *proximity* means MOST NEARLY   65.____

    A. similarity   B. exactness   C. harmony   D. nearness

66. His friends had a *detrimental* influence on him. The word detrimental means   66.____
    MOST NEARLY

    A. favorable   B. lasting   C. harmful   D. short-lived

67. The chief inspector relied upon the *veracity* of his inspectors. The word veracity means   67.____
    MOST NEARLY
    A. speed   B. assistance   C. shrewdness   D. truthfulness

68. There was much *diversity* in the suggestions submitted. The word diversity means   68.____
    MOST NEARLY

    A. similarity   B. value   C. triviality   D. variety

69. The survey was concerned with the problem of *indigence.* The word indigence means   69.____
    MOST NEARLY

    A. poverty   B. corruption   C. intolerance   D. morale

70. The investigator considered this evidence to be *extraneous.* The word extraneous   70.____
    means MOST NEARLY

    A. significant   B. pertinent but unobtainable
    C. not essential   D. inadequate

71. He was surppised at the *temerity* of the new employee. The word temerity means   71.____
    MOST NEARLY

    A. shyness   B. enthusiasm   C. rashness   D. self-control

72. The term *ex officio* means MOST NEARLY   72.____

    A. expelled from office
    B. a former holder of a high office
    C. without official approval
    D. by virtue of office or position

Questions 73-82.

DIRECTIONS: Questions 73 to 82 consist of four words each. One word in each row is
            INCORRECTLY spelled. For each item, print in the correspondingly numbered
            space at the right the letter preceding the word which is INCORRECTLY spelled.

73.   A. apparent   B. superintendent   C. releive   D. calendar   73.____

74.   A. foreign   B. negotiate   C. typical   D. discipline   74.____

75.   A. posponed   B. argument   C. susceptible D. deficit   75.____

76.   A. preferred   B. column   C. peculiar   D. equiped   76.____

15

77.	A. exaggerate	B. disatisfied	C. repetition	D. already	77._____
78.	A. livelihood	B. physician	C. obsticle	D. strategy	78._____
79.	A. courageous	B. ommission	C. ridiculous	D. awkward	79._____
80.	A. sincerely	B. abundance	C. negligable	D. elementary	80._____
81.	A. obsolete	B. mischievous	C. enumerate	D. atheletic	81._____
82.	A. fiscel	B. beneficiary	C. concede	D. translate	82._____

Questions 83-97

DIRECTIONS: Each of the following sentences may be classified MOST appropriately under one of the following four categories:
- A. faulty because of incorrect grammar
- B. faulty because of incorrect punctuation
- C. faulty because of incorrect capitalization
- D. correct

Examine each sentence carefully. Then, in the correspondingly numbered space at the right, print the letter preceding the option which is the BEST of the four suggested above. All incorrect sentences contain but one type of error. Consider a sentence correct if it contains none of the types of errors mentioned, even though there may be other eorrect ways of expressing the same thought.

83. Neither of the two administrators are going to attend the conference being held in Washington, D.C.   83._____

84. Since Miss Smith and Miss Jones have more experience than us, they have been given more responsible duties.   84._____

85. Mr. Shaw the supervisor of the stock room maintains an inventory of stationery and office supplies.   85._____

86. Inasmuch as this matter affects both you and I, we should take joint action.   86._____

87. Who do you think will be able to perform this highly technical work?   87._____

88. Of the two employees, John is considered the most competent.   88._____

89. He is not coming home on tuesday; we expect him next week.   89._____

90. Stenographers, as well as typists must be able to type rapidly and accurately.   90._____

91. Having been placed in the safe we were sure that the money would not be stolen   91._____

92. Only the employees who worked overtime last week may leave one hour earlier today.   92._____

93. We need someone who can speak french fluently.   93._____

94. A tall, elderly, man entered the office and asked to see Mr. Brown.   94._____

95. The clerk insisted that he had filed the correspondence in the proper cabinet.   95._____

96. "Will you assist us," he asked?   96.___

97. According to the information contained in the report, a large quantity of paper and   97.___
envelopes were used by this bureau last year.

Questions 98-100.

DIRECTIONS: Items 98 to 100 are a test of your proofreading ability.
Each item consists of Copy I and Copy II. You are to assume that Copy I in
each item is correct. Copy II, which is meant to be a duplicate of Copy I, may
contain some typographical errors.. In each item, compare Copy II with Copy
I and determine the number of errors in Copy II. If there are:
no errors, mark your answer A;
1 or 2 errors, mark your answer B;
3 or 4 errors, mark your answer C;
5 or 6 errors, mark your answer D;
7 errors or more, mark your answer E.

98. COPY I   98.___
The Commissioner, before issuing any such license, shall cause an investigation to be
made of the premises named and described in such application, to determine whether
all the provisions of the sanitary code, building code, state industrial code, state minimum
wage law, local laws, regulations of municipal agencies, and other requirements of this
article are fully observed. (Section B32-169.0 of Article 23.)

COPY II
The Commissioner, before issuing any such license shall cause an investigation to be
made of the premises named and described tn such applecation, to determine whether
all the provisions of the sanitary code, bilding code, state tndustrial code, state minimum
wage laws, local laws, regulations of municipal agencies, and other requirements of this
article are fully observed. (Section E32-169.0 of Article 23.)

99. COPY I   99.___
Among the persons who have been appointed to various agencies are John Queen,
9 West 55th Street, Brooklyn; Joseph Blount, 2497 Durward Road, Bronx; Lawrence
K. Eberhardt, 3194 Bedford Street, Manhattan; Reginald L. Darcy, 1476 Allerton Drive,
Bronx; and Benjamin Ledwith, 177 Greene Street, Manhattan.

COPY II
Among the persons who have been appointed to various agencies are John Queen,
9 West 56th Street,Brooklyn, Joseph Blount, 2497 Dureward Road, Bronx; Lawrence
K. Eberhart, 3194 Belford Street, Manhattan; Reginald L. Darcey, 1476 Allerton drive,
Bronx; and Benjamin Ledwith, 177 Green Street, Manhattan.

100. COPY I   100.___
Except as hereinafter provided, it shall be unlawful to use, store or have on hand any
inflammable motion picture film in quantities greater than one standard or two
sub-standard reels, or aggregating more than two thousand feet in length, or more than
ten pounds in weight without the permit required by this section.

COPY II
Except as herinafter provided, it shall be unlawfull to use, store or have on hand any
inflammable motion picture film, in quantities greater than one standard or two
substandard reels or aggregating more than two thousand feet in length, or more than
ten pounds in weight without the permit required by this section.

KEY (CORRECT ANSWERS)

1. C	26. D	51. C	76. D
2. D	27. A	52. C	77. B
3. B	28. C	53. B	78. C
4. D	29. D	54. C	79. B
5. A	30. C	55. A	80. C
6. B	31. A	56. C	81. D
7. C	32. C	57. D	82. A
8. C	33. B	58. C	83. A
9. A	34. D	59. B	84. A
10. B	35. B	60. D	85. B
11. A	36. B	61. A	86. A
12. C	37. C	62. D	87. D
13. D	38. A	63. B	88. A
14. A	39. B	64. B	89. C
15. B	40. B	65. D	90. B
16. D	41. D	66. C	91. A
17. C	42. A	67. D	92. D
18. B	43. D	68. D	93. C
19. C	44. B	69. A	94. B
20. D	45. C	70. C	95. D
21. B	46. B	71. C	96. B
22. A	47. A	72. D	97. A
23. A	48. A	73. C	98. D
24. D	49. C	74. D	99. E
25. B	50. B	75. A	100. E

DOCUMENTS AND FORMS
PREPARING WRITTEN MATERIALS
EXAMINATION SECTION
TEST 1

DIRECTIONS: Each question or incomplete statement is followed by several suggested answers or completions. Select the one that BEST answers the question or completes the statement. *PRINT THE LETTER OF THE CORRECT ANSWER IN THE SPACE AT THE RIGHT.*

1. Of the following forms, the one in which horizontal lines may BEST be omitted is one   1._____

    A. that is to be filled in by hand
    B. that is to be filled in by typewriter
    C. which requires many fill-ins
    D. with little room for fill-ins

2. A certain form letter starts with the words *Dear Mr.* followed by a blank space.   2._____
The MAJOR shortcoming in this is that

    A. salutations should not be placed on form letters
    B. *Gentlemen:* is preferable in a formal business letter
    C. the name will have to be typed in
    D. this salutation may be inappropriate

3. *Form paragraphs* may BEST be defined as   3._____

    A. block-style paragraphs
    B. paragraphs on a form
    C. paragraphs within a form letter
    D. standardized paragraphs used in correspondence

4. In general, the CHIEF economy of using multicopy forms is in   4._____

    A. the paper on which the form is printed
    B. printing the form
    C. employee time
    D. carbon paper

5. Suppose your supervisor has asked you to develop a form to record certain information   5._____
needed.
The FIRST thing you should do is to

    A. determine the type of data that will be recorded repeatedly so that it can be pre-printed
    B. study the relationship of the form to the job to be accomplished so that the form can be planned
    C. determine the information that will be recorded in the same place on each copy of the form so that it can be used as a check
    D. find out who will be responsible for supplying the information so that space can be provided for their signatures

6. Which of the following is MOST likely to reduce the volume of paperwork in a unit respon-   6.___
sible for preparing a large number of reports?

    A. Changing the office layout so that there will be a minimum of backtracking and delay
    B. Acquiring additional adding and calculating machines
    C. Consolidating some of the reports
    D. Inaugurating a *records retention* policy to reduce the length of time office papers are retained

7. Of the following basic guides to effective letter writing, which one would NOT be recom-   7.___
mended as a way of improving the quality of business letters?

    A. Use emphatic phrases like *close proximity* and *first and foremost* to round out sentences.
    B. Break up complicated sentences by making short sentences out of dependent clauses.
    C. Replace old-fashioned phrases like *enclosed please find* and *recent date* with a more direct approach.
    D. Personalize letters by using your reader's name at least once in the body of the message.

8. Suppose that you must write a reply letter to a citizen's request for a certain pamphlet   8.___
printed by your agency. The pamphlet is temporarily unavailable but a new supply will
be arriving by December 8 or 9.
Of the following four sentences, which one expresses the MOST positive business letter writing approach?

    A. We cannot send the materials you requested until after December 8.
    B. May we assure you that the materials you requested will be sent as quickly as possible.
    C. We will be sending the materials you requested as soon as our supply is replenished.
    D. We will mail the materials you requested on or shortly after December 8.

9. Using form letters in business correspondence is LEAST effective when   9.___

    A. answering letters on a frequently recurring subject
    B. giving the same information to many addresses
    C. the recipient is only interested in the routine information contained in the form letter
    D. a reply must be keyed to the individual requirements of the intended reader

10. The ability to write memos and letters is very important in clerical and administrative   10.___
work. Methodical planning of a reply letter usually involves the following basic steps
which are arranged in random order:
    I. Determine the purpose of the letter you are about to write.
    II. Make an outline of what information your reply letter should contain.
    III. Read carefully the letter to be answered to find out its main points.
    IV. Assemble the facts to be included in your reply letter.
    V. Visualize your intended reader and adapt your letter writing style to him.
If the above numbered steps were arranged in their proper logical order, the one which
would be THIRD in the sequence is

    A. II   B. III   C. IV   D. V

11. Generally, the frequency with which reports are to be submitted or the length of the inter-   11.____
val which they cover should depend MAINLY on the

    A. amount of time needed to prepare the reports
    B. degree of comprehensiveness required in the reports
    C. availability of the data to be included in the reports
    D. extent of the variations in the data with the passage of time

12. The objectiveness of a report is its unbiased presentation of the facts.   12.____
If this is so, which of the following reports listed below is likely to be the MOST objective?

    A. The Best Use of an Electronic Computer in Department Z
    B. The Case for Raising the Salaries of Employees in Department A
    C. Quarterly Summary of Production in the Duplicating Unit of Department Y
    D. Recommendation to Terminate Employee X's Services Because of Misconduct

13. Of the following, the MOST effective report writing style is usually characterized by   13.____

    A. covering all the main ideas in the same paragraph
    B. presenting each significant point in a new paragraph
    C. placing the least important points before the most important points
    D. giving all points equal emphasis throughout the report

14. Of the following, which factor is COMMON to all types of reports?   14.____

    A. Presentation of information
    B. Interpretation of findings
    C. Chronological ordering of the information
    D. Presentation of conclusions and recommendations

15. When writing a report, the one of the following which you should do FIRST is   15.____

    A. set up a logical work schedule
    B. determine your objectives in writing the report
    C. select your statistical material
    D. obtain the necessary data from the files

16. Good report writing utilizes, where possible, the use of table of contents, clear titles and   16.____
sub-titles, well-labeled tables and figures, and good summaries in prominent places.
These features in a report are MOST helpful in

    A. saving the reader's time
    B. emphasizing objectivity
    C. providing a basic reference tool
    D. forming a basis for future action

17. The one of the following which BEST describes a periodic report is that it   17.____

    A. provides a record of accomplishments for a given time span and a comparison with
       similar time spans in the past
    B. covers the progress made in a project that has been postponed
    C. integrates, summarizes, and perhaps interprets published data on technical or sci-
       entific material
    D. describes a decision, advocates a policy or action, and presents facts in support of
       the writer's position

18. The PRIMARY purpose of including pictorial illustrations in a formal report is usually to   18.___

    A.   amplify information which has been adequately treated verbally
    B.   present details that are difficult to describe verbally
    C.   provide the reader with a pleasant, momentary distraction
    D.   present supplementary information incidental to the main ideas developed in the report

19. Of the following, which is usually the MOST important guideline in writing business letters?   19.___
A letter should be

    A.   Neat
    B.   Written in a formalized style
    C.   Written in clear language intelligible to the reader
    D.   Written in the past tense

20. Suppose you are asked to edit a policy statement. You note that personal pronouns like   20.___
you, we, and *I* are used freely.
Which of the following statements BEST applies to this use of personal pronouns?

    A.   It is proper usage because written business language should not be different from carefully spoken business language.
    B.   It requires correction because it is ungrammatical.
    C.   It is proper because it is clearer and has a warmer tone.
    D.   It requires correction because policies should be expressed in an impersonal manner.

21. Good business letters are coherent.   21.___
To be coherent means to

    A.   keep only one unifying idea in the message
    B.   present the total message
    C.   use simple, direct words for the message
    D.   tie together the various ideas in the message

22. A functional forms file is a collection of forms which are grouped by   22.___

    A.   purpose   B.   department   C.   title   D.   subject

23. All of the following are reasons to consult a records retention schedule except one.   23.___
Which one is that?
To determine

    A.   Whether something should be filed
    B.   How long something should stay in file
    C.   Who should be assigned to filing
    D.   When something on file should be destroyed

24. A secretary is MOST likely to employ a form letter when

    A. an answer is not required
    B. the same information must be repeated from letter to letter
    C. there is not enough information to write a detailed reply
    D. varied correspondence must be sent out quickly

24.____

25. Of the following, the BASIC intent of naming a form is to provide the means to

    A. code those factors recorded on each form
    B. describe the use of the form
    C. index each form
    D. call attention to specific sections within each form

25.____

KEY (CORRECT ANSWERS)

1.	B		11.	D
2.	D		12.	C
3.	D		13.	B
4.	C		14.	A
5.	B		15.	B
6.	C		16.	A,C
7.	A		17.	A
8.	D		18.	B
9.	D		19.	C
10.	A		20.	D

21.	D
22.	A
23.	C
24.	B
25.	B

TEST 2

Each question or incomplete statement is followed by several suggested answers or completions. Select the one that BEST answers the question or completes the statement. *PRINT THE LETTER OF THE CORRECT ANSWER IN THE SPACE AT THE RIGHT.*

1. Assume that you are assigned the task of reducing the time and costs involved in completing a form that is frequently used in your agency. After analyzing the matter, you decide to reduce the writing requirements of the form through the use of ballot boxes and preprinted data.
   If exact copy-to-copy registration of this form is necessary, it is MOST advisable to

   A. vary the sizes of the ballot boxes
   B. stagger the ballot boxes
   C. place the ballot boxes as close together as possible
   D. have the ballot boxes follow the captions

   1.___

2. To overcome problems that are involved in the use of cut-sheet and padded forms, specialty forms have been developed. Normally, these forms are commercially manufactured rather than produced in-plant. Before designing a form as a specialty form, however, you should be assured that certain factors are present.
   Which one of the following factors deserve LEAST consideration?

   A. The form is to be used in quantities of 5,000 or more annually.
   B. The forms will be prepared on equipment using either a pinfeed device or pressure rollers for continuous feed-through.
   C. Two or more copies of the form set must be held together for further processing subsequent to the initial distribution of the form set.
   D. Copies of the form will be identical, and no items of data will be selectively eliminated from one or more copies of the form.

   2.___

3. Although a well-planned form should require little explanation as to its completion, there are many occasions when the analyst will find it necessary to include instructions on the form to assure that the person completing it does so correctly.
   With respect to such instructions, it is usually considered to be LEAST appropriate to place them

   A. in footnotes at the bottom of the form
   B. following the spaces to be completed
   C. directly under the form's title
   D. on the front of the form

   3.___

4. One of the basic data-arrangement methods used in forms design is the *on-line* method. When this method is used, captions appear on the same line as the space provided for entry of the variable data.
   This arrangement is NOT recommended because it

   A. forces the typist to make use of the typewriter's tab stops, thus increasing processing time
   B. wastes horizontal space since the caption appears on the writing line
   C. tends to make the variable data become more dominant than the captions
   D. increases the form's processing time by requiring the typist to continually roll the platen back and forth to expose the caption

   4.___

5. Of the following, the BEST reason for using form letters in correspondence is that they are   5.____

    A. concise and businesslike
    B. impersonal in tone
    C. uniform in appearance
    D. economical for large mailings

6. Of the following, the MOST important reason to sort large volumes of documents before filing is that sorting   6.____

    A. decreases the need for cross-referencing
    B. eliminates the need to keep the files up to date
    C. prevents overcrowding of the file drawers
    D. saves time and energy in filing

7. To overcome the manual collation problem, forms are frequently padded.
Of the following statements which relate to this type of packaging, select the one that is MOST accurate.   7.____

    A. Typewritten forms which are prepared as padded forms are more efficient than all other packaging.
    B. Padded forms are best suited for handwritten forms.
    C. It is difficult for a printer to pad form copies of different colors.
    D. Registration problems increase when cut-sheet forms are padded.

8. Most forms are cut from a standard mill sheet of paper. This is the size on which forms dealers base their prices. Since an agency is paying for a full-size sheet of paper, it is the responsibility of the analyst to design forms so that as many as possible may be cut from the sheet without waste.
Of the following sizes, select the one that will cut from a standard mill sheet with the GREATEST waste and should, therefore, be avoided if possible.   8.____

    A. 4" x 6"   B. 5" x 8"   C. 9" x 12"   D. $8\frac{1}{2}$" x 14"

9. Assume that the work in your department involves the use of many technical terms.
In such a situation, when you are answering inquiries from the general public, it would usually be BEST to   9.____

    A. use simple language and avoid the technical terms
    B. use the technical terms whenever possible
    C. use technical terms freely, but explain each term in parentheses
    D. apologize if you are forced to use a technical term

10. You are answering a letter that was written on the letterhead of the ABC Company and signed by James H. Block, Treasurer.
What is usually considered to be the CORRECT salutation to use in your reply?
Dear   10.____

    A. ABC Company: B. Sirs:
    C. Mr. Block: D. Mr. Treasurer:

11. Assume that one of your duties is to handle routine letters of inquiry from the public. The one of the following which is usually considered to be MOST desirable in replying to such a letter is a

    A. detailed answer handwritten on the original letter of inquiry
    B. phone call since you can cover details more easily over the phone than in a letter
    C. short letter giving the specific information requested
    D. long letter discussing all possible aspects of the questions raised

11.___

12. The CHIEF reason for dividing a letter into paragraphs is to

    A. make the message clear to the reader by starting a new paragraph for each new topic
    B. make a short letter occupy as much of the page as possible
    C. keep the reader's attention by providing a pause from time to time
    D. make the letter look neat and businesslike

12.___

13. An *Attention* line is used in correspondence to

    A. indicate to the person receiving the correspondence that it contains an enclosure
    B. direct correspondence addressed to an organization to a particular individual within the organization
    C. greet the recipient of the correspondence
    D. highlight the main concern of the correspondence

13.___

14. In deciding upon the advisability of recording certain information on a regular basis, the MOST important consideration is:

    A. How much will it cost?
    B. Is it necessary?
    C. Is space available for keeping additional records?
    D. Will it fit into the work pattern?

14.___

15. Instructions for filling out simple forms should USUALLY appear

    A. at the bottom of the form
    B. on a separate sheet of instructions
    C. on the reverse side of the form
    D. with the items to which they refer

15.___

16. Each new form should be given a number PRIMARILY because

    A. it provides a means of easy reference
    B. names are not sufficiently descriptive
    C. numbering forms is common government practice
    D. numbers are more suitable for automatic data processing

16.___

17. Of the following, the MOST important features of an effective business letter are

    A. introduction and conclusion
    B. punctuation and paragraphing
    C. simplicity and clarity
    D. style and organization

17.___

18. When recording receipt of purchases of equipment, the one of the following which is usu-   18.____
ally LEAST important is

    A. identification of the item
    B. name of the vendor
    C. quantity of the item
    D. weight of the item

19. In deciding which data should be collected for permanent records, the MOST important   19.____
consideration is the

    A. amount of data available
    B. ease of processing the different types of data
    C. type of record-keeping system involved
    D. use to which such data may be put

20. In a certain filing system, documents are consecutively numbered as they are filed, a   20.____
register is maintained of such consecutively numbered documents, and a record is kept
of the number of each document removed from the files and its destination.
This system will NOT help in

    A. finding the present whereabouts of a particular document
    B. proving the accuracy of the data recorded on a certain document
    C. indicating whether observed existing documents were ever filed
    D. locating a desired document without knowing what its contents are

21. The inside address in a business letter indicates to whom the letter is to be sent.   21.____
Of the following, the MOST important reason why a letter should contain the inside
address is that the inside address

    A. gives the letter a personal, friendly tone
    B. simplifies the work of dictation and transcription
    C. gives the letter a balanced appearance
    D. identifies the addressee when the envelope containing the letter is discarded

22. The appearance of a business letter should make a favorable first impression on the per-   22.____
son to whom the letter is sent.
In order to make such an impression, it is LEAST important that the

    A. letter be centered on the page
    B. margins be as even as possible
    C. letter make a neat appearance
    D. paragraphs be of the same length

23. A typed rough draft of a report should be double-spaced and should have wide margins   23.____
PRIMARILY in order to

    A. estimate the number of pages the report will contain
    B. allow space for making corrections in the report
    C. determine whether the report is well-organized
    D. make the report easy to read

24. Suppose that you are assigned to make a number of original typewritten copies of a printed report. In doing this assignment, you type the first copy from the printed report and then type each subsequent copy from the last one you prepared.
You could be MOST certain that there were no errors made in the copies if you found no errors when comparing the

    24.___

   A. printed report with any one of the copies
   B. first copy with the printed report
   C. last copy with the printed report
   D. first copy with the last copy

25. Before typing on more than one copy of a printed form, the one of the following which you should do FIRST is to

    25.___

   A. align the type so that the tails of the longer letters will rest on the lines printed on the form
   B. check the alignment of the copies of the forms by holding them up to the light
   C. insert the carbon paper into the typewriter and then insert the copies of the form
   D. insert the copies of the form into the typewriter and then insert the carbon paper

———

KEY (CORRECT ANSWERS)

1.	B		11.	C
2.	D		12.	A
3.	A		13.	B
4.	B		14.	B
5.	D		15.	D
6.	D		16.	A
7.	B		17.	C
8.	C		18.	D
9.	A		19.	D
10.	C		20.	B

21.	D
22.	D
23.	B
24.	C
25.	B

———

TEST 3

DIRECTIONS: Each question or incomplete statement is followed by several suggested answers or completions. Select the one that BEST answers the question or completes the statement. *PRINT THE LETTER OF THE CORRECT ANSWER IN THE SPACE AT THE RIGHT.*

1. The supervisor who makes a special point of using long words in preparing written reports is, in general, PROBABLY being

    A. *unwise* because a written report should be factual and accurate
    B. *unwise* because simplicity in a report is usually desirable
    C. *wise* because the written report will become a permanent record
    D. *wise* because with long words he can use the right emphasis in his report

1.____

2. Before you turn in a report you have written of an investigation that you made, you discover some additional information that you didn't know about before.
Whether or not you rewrite your report to include this additional information should depend MAINLY on the

    A. amount of time left in which to submit the report
    B. effect this information will have on the conclusions of the report
    C. number of changes that you will have to make in your original report
    D. possibility of turning in a supplementary report later

2.____

3. When an applicant is approved for public assistance, the supervising clerk must fill in standard forms with certain information.
The GREATEST advantage of using standard forms in this situation rather than having the supervising clerk write the report as he sees fit is that

    A. the report can be acted on quickly
    B. the report can be written without directions from a supervisor
    C. needed information is less likely to be left out of the report
    D. information that is written up this way is more likely to be verified

3.____

4. In some types of reports, visual aids add interest, meaning, and support. They also provide an essential means of effectively communicating the message of the report.
Of the following, the selection of the suitable visual aids to use with a report is LEAST dependent on the

    A. nature and scope of the report
    B. way in which the aid is to be used
    C. aids used in other reports
    D. prospective readers of the report

4.____

5. A report is often revised several times before final preparation and distribution in an effort to make certain the report meets the needs of the situation for which it is designed.
Which of the following is the BEST way for the author to be sure that a report covers the areas he intended?

    A. Obtain a co-worker's opinion
    B. Compare it with a content checklist
    C. Test it on a subordinate
    D. Check his bibliography

5.____

6. Visual aids used in a report may be placed either in the text material or in the appendix. Deciding where to put a chart, table, or any such aid should depend on the   6.___

    A. title of the report   B. purpose of the visual aid
    C. title of the visual aid   D. length of the report

7. In which of the following situations is an oral report PREFERABLE to a written report? When a(n)   7.___

    A. recommendation is being made for a future plan of action
    B. department head requests immediate information
    C. long-standing policy change is made
    D. analysis of complicated statistical data is involved

8. All of the following rules will aid in producing clarity in report writing EXCEPT: 8.___

    A. Give specific details or examples, if possible
    B. Keep related words close together in each sentence
    C. Present information in sequential order
    D. Put several thoughts or ideas in each paragraph

9. When preparing a long report on a study prepared for your superior, the one of the following which should usually come FIRST in your report is a(n)   9.___

    A. brief description of the working procedure followed in your study
    B. review of the background conditions leading to the study
    C. summary of your conclusions
    D. outline of suggested procedures for implementing the report

10. The MAIN function of a research report is usually to   10.___

    A. convince the reader of the adequacy of the research
    B. report as expeditiously as possible what was done, why it was done, the results, and the conclusions
    C. contribute to the body of scientific knowledge
    D. substantiate an a priori conclusion by presenting a set of persuasive quantitative data

11. Words in a sentence must be arranged properly to make sure that the intended meaning of the sentence is clear. The sentence below that does NOT make sense because a clause has been separated from the word on which its meaning depends is: 11.___

    A. To be a good writer, clarity is necessary.
    B. To be a good writer, you must write clearly.
    C. You must write clearly to be a good writer.
    D. Clarity is necessary to good writing.

12. The use of a graph to show statistical data in a report is SUPERIOR to a table because it   12.___

    A. emphasizes approximations
    B. emphasizes facts and relationships more dramatically
    C. presents data more accurately
    D. is easily understood by the average reader

13. Of the following, the degree of formality required of a written report prepared by a labor relations specialist is MOST likely to depend on the   13.____

    A. subject matter of the report
    B. frequency of its occurrence
    C. amount of time available for its preparation
    D. audience for whom the report is intended

14. Of the following, a DISTINGUISHING characteristic of a written report intended for the head of your agency as compared to a report prepared for a lower-echelon staff member is that the report for the agency should usually include   14.____

    A. considerably more detail, especially statistical data
    B. the essential details in an abbreviated form
    C. all available source material
    D. an annotated bibliography

15. Assume that you are asked to write a lengthy report for use by the administrator of your agency, the subject of which is *The Impact of Proposed New Data Processing Operations on Line Personnel* in your agency. You decide that the most appropriate type of report for you to prepare is an analytical report, including recommendations.
The MAIN reason for your decision is that   15.____

    A. the subject of the report is extremely complex
    B. large sums of money are involved
    C. the report is being prepared for the administrator
    D. you intend to include charts and graphs

16. Assume that you are preparing a report based on a survey dealing with the attitudes of employees in Division X regarding proposed new changes in compensating employees for working overtime. Three percent of the respondents to the survey voluntarily offer an unfavorable opinion on the method of assigning overtime work, a question not specifically asked of the employees.
On the basis of this information, the MOST appropriate and significant of the following comments for you to make in the report with regard to employees' attitudes on assigning overtime work is that   16.____

    A. an insignificant percentage of employees dislike the method of assigning overtime work
    B. three percent of the employees in Division X dislike the method of assigning overtime work
    C. three percent of the sample selected for the survey voiced an unfavorable opinion on the method of assigning overtime work
    D. some employees voluntarily voiced negative feelings about the method of assigning overtime work, making it impossible to determine the extent of this attitude

17. Four parts of a survey report are listed below, not necessarily in their proper order: 17.____
    I. Body of report
    II. Synopsis of report
    III. Letter of transmittal
    IV. Conclusions
Which one of the following represents the BEST sequence for inclusion of these parts in a report?

    A. III, IV, I, II   B. II, I, III, IV   C. III, II, I, IV   D. I, III, IV, II

18. Of the following, the MOST important value of a good report is that it   18.___

    A. reflects credit upon the person who submitted the report
    B. provides good reference material
    C. expedites official business
    D. expresses the need for official action

19. The MOST important requirement in report writing is   19.___

    A. promptness in turning in reports
    B. length
    C. grammatical construction
    D. accuracy

20. You have discovered an error in your report submitted to the main office.   20.___
You should

    A. wait until the error is discovered in the main office and then correct it
    B. go directly to the supervisor in the main office after working hours and ask him unofficially to correct the answer
    C. notify the main office immediately so that the error can be corrected if necessary
    D. do nothing since it is possible that one error will have little effect on the total report

21. When you determine the methods of emphasis you will use in typing the titles, headings,   21.___
and subheadings of a report, the one of the following which it is MOST important to keep
in mind is that

    A. all headings of the same rank should be typed in the same way
    B. all headings should be typed in the single style which is most pleasing to the eye
    C. headings should not take up more than one-third of the page width
    D. only one method should be used for all headings, whatever their rank

22. Proper division of a letter into paragraphs requires that the writer of business letters   22.___
should, as much as possible, be sure that

    A. each paragraph is short
    B. each paragraph develops discussion of just one topic
    C. each paragraph repeats the theme of the total message
    D. there are at least two paragraphs for every message

23. An editor is given a letter with this initial paragraph: 23.___
*We have received your letter, which we read with interest, and we are happy to
respond to your question. In fact, we talked with several people in our office to get
ideas to send to you.*
Which of the following is it MOST reasonable for the editor to conclude?
The paragraph is

    A. concise
    B. communicating something of value
    C. unnecessary
    D. coherent

24. In preparing a report that includes several tables, if not otherwise instructed, the typist should MOST properly include a list of tables

    24._____

    A. in the introductory part of the report
    B. at the end of each chapter in the body of the report
    C. in the supplementary part of the report as an appendix
    D. in the supplementary part of the report as a part of the index

25. You have been asked to write a report on methods of hiring and training new employees. Your report is going to be about ten pages long.
For the convenience of your readers, a brief summary of your findings should

    25._____

    A. appear at the beginning of your report
    B. be appended to the report as a postscript
    C. be circulated in a separate memo
    D. be inserted in tabular form in the middle of your report

26. A new student program is being set up for which certain new forms will be needed. You have been asked to design these forms.
Of the following, the FIRST step you should take in planning the forms is

    26._____

    A. finding out the exact purpose for which each form will be used
    B. deciding what size of paper should be used for each form
    C. determining whether multiple copies will be needed for any of the forms
    D. setting up a new filing system to handle the new forms

27. Many government agencies require the approval by a central forms control unit of the design and reproduction of new office forms.
The one of the following results of this procedure that is a DISADVANTAGE is that requiring prior approval of a central forms control unit usually

    27._____

    A. limits the distribution of forms to those offices with justifiable reasons for receiving them
    B. permits checking whether existing forms or modifications of them are in line with current agency needs
    C. encourages reliance on only the central office to set up all additional forms when needed
    D. provides for someone with a specialized knowledge of forms design to review and criticize new and revised forms

28. Suppose that you are assigned to prepare a form from which certain information will be posted in a ledger.
It would be MOST helpful to the person posting the information in the ledger if, in designing the form, you were to

    28._____

    A. use the same color paper for both the form and the ledger
    B. make the form the same size as the pages of the ledger
    C. have the information on the form in the same order as that used in the ledger
    D. include in the form a box which is to be initialed when the data on the form have been posted in the ledger

29. In the effective design of office forms, the FIRST step to take is to   29.___

    A. decide what information should be included
    B. decide the purpose for which the form will be used
    C. identify the form by name and number
    D. identify the employees who will be using the form

30. Some designers of office forms prefer to locate the instructions on how to fill out the form   30.___
at the bottom of it.
The MOST logical objection to placing such instructions at the bottom of the form is
that

    A. instructions at the bottom require an excess of space
    B. all form instructions should be outlined with a separate paragraph
    C. the form may be partly filled out before the instructions are seen
    D. the bottom of the form should be reserved only for authorization and signature

———

KEY (CORRECT ANSWERS)

1.	B	11.	A	21.	A
2.	B	12.	B	22.	B
3.	C	13.	D	23.	C
4.	C	14.	B	24.	A
5.	B	15.	A	25.	A
6.	B	16.	D	26.	A
7.	B	17.	C	27.	C
8.	D	18.	C	28.	C
9.	C	19.	D	29.	B
10.	B	20.	C	30.	C

———

CLERICAL ABILITIES

EXAMINATION SECTION
TEST 1

DIRECTIONS: Each question or incomplete statement is followed by several suggested answers or completions. Select the one that BEST answers the question or completes the statement. *PRINT THE LETTER OF THE CORRECT ANSWER IN THE SPACE AT THE RIGHT.*

Questions 1-4.

DIRECTIONS: Questions 1 through 4 are to be answered on the basis of the information given below.

The most commonly used filing system and the one that is easiest to learn is alphabetical filing. This involves putting records in an A to Z order, according to the letters of the alphabet. The name of a person is filed by using the following order: first, the surname or last name; second, the first name; third, the middle name or middle initial. For example, *Henry C. Young* is filed under *Y* and thereafter under *Young, Henry C.* The name of a company is filed in the same way. For example, *Long Cabinet Co.* is filed under *L,* while *John T. Long Cabinet Co.* is filed under *L* and thereafter under *Long., John T. Cabinet Co.*

1. The one of the following which lists the names of persons in the CORRECT alphabetical order is: 1.____

    A. Mary Carrie, Helen Carrol, James Carson, John Carter
    B. James Carson, Mary Carrie, John Carter, Helen Carrol
    C. Helen Carrol, James Carson, John Carter, Mary Carrie
    D. John Carter, Helen Carrol, Mary Carrie, James Carson

2. The one of the following which lists the names of persons in the CORRECT alphabetical order is: 2.____

    A. Jones, John C.; Jones, John A.; Jones, John P.; Jones, John K.
    B. Jones, John P.; Jones, John K.; Jones, John C.; Jones, John A.
    C. Jones, John A.; Jones, John C.; Jones, John K.; Jones, John P.
    D. Jones, John K.; Jones, John C.; Jones, John A.; Jones, John P.

3. The one of the following which lists the names of the companies in the CORRECT alphabetical order is: 3.____

    A. Blane Co., Blake Co., Block Co., Blear Co.
    B. Blake Co., Blane Co., Blear Co., Block Co.
    C. Block Co., Blear Co., Blane Co., Blake Co.
    D. Blear Co., Blake Co., Blane Co., Block Co.

4. You are to return to the file an index card on *Barry C. Wayne Materials and Supplies Co.* Of the following, the CORRECT alphabetical group that you should return the index card to is   4.____

    A. A to G   B. H to M   C. N to S   D. T to Z

Questions 5-10.

DIRECTIONS: In each of Questions 5 through 10, the names of four people are given. For each question, choose as your answer the one of the four names given which should be filed FIRST according to the usual system of alphabetical filing of names, as described in the following paragraph.

In filing names, you must start with the last name. Names are filed in order of the first letter of the last name, then the second letter, etc. Therefore, BAILY would be filed before BROWN, which would be filed before COLT. A name with fewer letters of the same type comes first; i.e., Smith before Smithe. If the last names are the same, the names are filed alphabetically by the first name. If the first name is an initial, a name with an initial would come before a first name that starts with the same letter as the initial. Therefore, I. BROWN would come before IRA BROWN. Finally, if both last name and first name are the same, the name would be filed alphabetically by the middle name, once again an initial coming before a middle name which starts with the same letter as the initial. If there is no middle name at all, the name would come before those with middle initials or names.

Sample Question: A.   Lester Daniels
                   B.   William Dancer
                   C.   Nathan Danzig
                   D.   Dan Lester

The last names beginning with D are filed before the last name beginning with L. Since DANIELS, DANCER, and DANZIG all begin with the same three letters, you must look at the fourth letter of the last name to determine which name should be filed first. C comes before I or Z in the alphabet, so DANCER is filed before DANIELS or DANZIG. Therefore, the answer to the above sample question is B.

5.   A.   Scott Biala   5.____
     B.   Mary Byala
     C.   Martin Baylor
     D.   Francis Bauer

6.   A.   Howard J. Black   6.____
     B.   Howard Black
     C.   J. Howard Black
     D.   John H. Black

7.   A.   Theodora Garth Kingston   7.____
     B.   Theadore Barth Kingston
     C.   Thomas Kingston
     D.   Thomas T. Kingston

8.   A.   Paulette Mary Huerta   8.____
     B.   Paul M. Huerta
     C.   Paulette L. Huerta
     D.   Peter A. Huerta

9. A. Martha Hunt Morgan
    B. Martin Hunt Morgan
    C. Mary H. Morgan
    D. Martine H. Morgan

9._____

10. A. James T. Meerschaum
    B. James M. Mershum
    C. James F. Mearshaum
    D. James N. Meshum

10._____

Questions 11-14.

DIRECTIONS: Questions 11 through 14 are to be answered SOLELY on the basis of the following information.

You are required to file various documents in file drawers which are labeled according to the following pattern:

DOCUMENTS

MEMOS		LETTERS	
File	Subject	File	Subject
84PM1 - (A-L)		84PC1 - (A-L)	
84PM2 - (M-Z)		84PC2 - (M-Z)	

REPORTS		INQUIRIES	
File	Subject	File	Subject
84PR1 - (A-L)		84PQ1 - (A-L)	
84PR2 - (M-Z)		84PQ2 - (M-Z)	

11. A letter dealing with a burglary should be filed in the drawer labeled

    A. 84PM1   B. 84PC1   C. 84PR1   D. 84PQ2

11._____

12. A report on Statistics should be found in the drawer labeled

    A. 84PM1   B. 84PC2   C. 84PR2   D. 84PQ2

12._____

13. An inquiry is received about parade permit procedures. It should be filed in the drawer labeled

    A. 84PM2   B. 84PC1   C. 84PR1   D. 84PQ2

13._____

14. A police officer has a question about a robbery report you filed.
    You should pull this file from the drawer labeled

    A. 84PM1   B. 84PM2   C. 84PR1   D. 84PR2

14._____

Questions 15-22.

DIRECTIONS: Each of Questions 15 through 22 consists of four or six numbered names. For each question, choose the option (A, B, C, or D) which indicates the order in which the names should be filed in accordance with the following filing instructions:
- File alphabetically according to last name, then first name, then middle initial.
- File according to each successive letter within a name.

- When comparing two names in which, the letters in the longer name are identical to the corresponding letters in the shorter name, the shorter name is filed first.
- When the last names are the same, initials are always filed before names beginning with the same letter.

15.   I.   Ralph Robinson   15.___
           II.   Alfred Ross
          III. Luis Robles
          IV. James Roberts

The CORRECT filing sequence for the above names should be

  A. IV, II, I, III   B. I, IV, III, II
  C. III, IV, I, II   D. IV, I, III, II

16.   I.   Irwin Goodwin   16.___
           II.   Inez Gonzalez
          III. Irene Goodman
          IV. Ira S. Goodwin
          V.   Ruth I. Goldstein
          VI. M.B. Goodman

The CORRECT filing sequence for the above names should be

  A. V, II, I, IV, III, VI   B. V, II, VI, III, IV, I
  C. V, II, III, VI, IV, I   D. V, II, III, VI, I, IV

17.   I.   George Allan   17.___
           II.   Gregory Allen
          III. Gary Allen
          IV. George Allen

The CORRECT filing sequence for the above names should be

  A. IV, III, I, II   B. I, IV, II, III
  C. III, IV, I, II   D. I, III, IV, II

18.   I.   Simon Kauffman   18.___
           II.   Leo Kaufman
          III. Robert Kaufmann
          IV. Paul Kauffmann

The CORRECT filing sequence for the above names should be

  A. I, IV, II, III   B. II, IV, III, I
  C. III, II, IV, I   D. I, II, III, IV

19.   I.   Roberta Williams   19.___
           II.   Robin Wilson
          III. Roberta Wilson
          IV. Robin Williams

The CORRECT filing sequence for the above names should be

  A. III, II, IV, I   B. I, IV, III, II
  C. I, II, III, IV   D. III, I, II, IV

20.
    I.   Lawrence Shultz
    II. Albert Schultz
    III. Theodore Schwartz
    IV. Thomas Schwarz
    V. Alvin Schultz
    VI. Leonard Shultz

The CORRECT filing sequence for the above names should be

A. II, V, III, IV, I, VI   B. IV, III, V, I, II, VI
C. II, V, I, VI, III, IV   D. I, VI, II, V, III, IV

20._____

21.
    I.   McArdle
    II. Mayer
    III. Maletz
    IV. McNiff
    V. Meyer
    VI. MacMahon

The CORRECT filing sequence for the above names should be

A. I, IV, VI, III, II, V   B. II, I, IV, VI, III, V
C. VI, III, II, I, IV, V   D. VI, III, II, V, I, IV

21._____

22.
    I.   Jack E. Johnson
    II. R.H. Jackson
    III. Bertha Jackson
    IV. J.T. Johnson
    V. Ann Johns
    VI. John Jacobs

The CORRECT filing sequence for the above names should be

A. II, III, VI, V, IV, I   B. III, II, VI, V, IV, I
C. VI, II, III, I, V, IV   D. III, II, VI, IV, V, I

22._____

Questions 23-30.

DIRECTIONS: The code table below shows 10 letters with matching numbers. For each question, there are three sets of letters. Each set of letters is followed by a set of numbers which may or may not match their correct letter according to the code table. For each question, check all three sets of letters and numbers and mark your answer:

    A. if no pairs are correctly matched
    B. if only one pair is correctly matched
    C. if only two pairs are correctly matched
    D. if all three pairs are correctly matched

CODE TABLE

T	M	V	D	S	P	R	G	B	H
1	2	3	4	5	6	7	8	9	0

Sample Question: TMVDSP - 123456
                        RGBHTM - 789011
                        DSPRGB - 256789

In the sample question above, the first set of numbers correctly matches its set of letters. But the second and third pairs contain mistakes. In the second pair, M is incorrectly matched with number 1. According to the code table, letter M should be correctly matched with number 2. In the third pair, the letter D is incorrectly matched with number 2. According to the code table, letter D should be correctly matched with number 4. Since only one of the pairs is correctly matched, the answer to this sample question is B.

23.   RSBMRM 759262   23._____
      GDSRVH 845730
      VDBRTM 349713

24.   TGVSDR 183247   24._____
      SMHRDP 520647
      TRMHSR 172057

25.   DSPRGM 456782   25._____
      MVDBHT 234902
      HPMDBT 062491

26.   BVPTRD 936184   26._____
      GDPHMB 807029
      GMRHMV 827032

27.   MGVRSH 283750   27._____
      TRDMBS 174295
      SPRMGV 567283

28.   SGBSDM 489542   28._____
      MGHPTM 290612
      MPBMHT 269301

29.   TDPBHM 146902   29._____
      VPBMRS 369275
      GDMBHM 842902

30.   MVPTBV 236194   30._____
      PDRTMB 647128
      BGTMSM 981232

KEY (CORRECT ANSWERS)

1.	A	11.	B	21.	C
2.	C	12.	C	22.	B
3.	B	13.	D	23.	B
4.	D	14.	D	24.	B
5.	D	15.	D	25.	C
6.	B	16.	C	26.	A
7.	B	17.	D	27.	D
8.	B	18.	A	28.	A
9.	A	19.	B	29.	D
10.	C	20.	A	30.	A

———

TEST 2

DIRECTIONS: Each question or incomplete statement is followed by several suggested answers or completions. Select the one that BEST answers the question or completes the statement. *PRINT THE LETTER OF THE CORRECT ANSWER IN THE SPACE AT THE RIGHT.*

Questions 1-10.

DIRECTIONS: Questions 1 through 10 each consists of two columns, each containing four lines of names, numbers and/or addresses. For each question, compare the lines in Column I with the lines in Column II to see if they match exactly, and mark your answer A, B, C, or D, according to the following instructions:
- A. all four lines match exactly
- B. only three lines match exactly
- C. only two lines match exactly
- D. only one line matches exactly

	COLUMN I	COLUMN II	
1.	I. Earl Hodgson II. 1409870 III. Shore Ave. IV. Macon Rd.	Earl Hodgson 1408970 Schore Ave. Macon Rd.	1.___
2.	I. 9671485 II. 470 Astor Court III. Halprin, Phillip IV. Frank D. Poliseo	9671485 470 Astor Court Halperin, Phillip Frank D. Poliseo	2.___
3.	I. Tandem Associates II. 144-17 Northern Blvd. III. Alberta Forchi IV. Kings Park, NY 10751	Tandom Associates 144-17 Northern Blvd. Albert Forchi Kings Point, NY 10751	3.___
4.	I. Bertha C. McCormack II. Clayton, MO. III. 976-4242 IV. New City, NY 10951	Bertha C. McCormack Clayton, MO. 976-4242 New City, NY 10951	4.___
5.	I. George C. Morill II. Columbia, SC 29201 III. Louis Ingham IV. 3406 Forest Ave.	George C. Morrill Columbia, SD 29201 Louis Ingham 3406 Forest Ave.	5.___
6.	I. 506 S. Elliott Pl. II. Herbert Hall III. 4712 Rockaway Pkway IV. 169 E. 7 St.	506 S. Elliott Pl. Hurbert Hall 4712 Rockaway Pkway 169 E. 7 St.	6.___

	COLUMN I	COLUMN II	

7.
I. 345 Park Ave.   345 Park Pl.   7.____
II. Colman Oven Corp.   Coleman Oven Corp.
III. Robert Conte   Robert Conti
IV. 6179846   6179846

8.
I. Grigori Schierber   Grigori Schierber   8.____
II. Des Moines, Iowa   Des Moines, Iowa
III. Gouverneur Hospital   Gouverneur Hospital
IV. 91-35 Cresskill Pl.   91-35 Cresskill Pl.

9.
I. Jeffery Janssen   Jeffrey Janssen   9.____
II. 8041071   8041071
III. 40 Rockefeller Plaza   40 Rockafeller Plaza
IV. 407 6 St.   406 7 St.

10.
I. 5971996   5871996   10.____
II. 3113 Knickerbocker Ave.   3113 Knickerbocker Ave.
III. 8434 Boston Post Rd.   8424 Boston Post Rd.
IV. Penn Station   Penn Station

Questions 11-14.

DIRECTIONS: Questions 11 through 14 are to be answered by looking at the four groups of names and addresses listed below (I, II, III, and IV) and then finding out the number of groups that have their corresponding numbered lines exactly the same.

GROUP I
Line 1. Richmond General Hospital
Line 2. Geriatric Clinic
Line 3. 3975 Paerdegat St.
Line 4 Loudonville, New York 11538

GROUP II
Richman General Hospital
Geriatric Clinic
3975 Peardegat St.
Londonville, New York 11538

GROUP III
Line 1. Richmond General Hospital
Line 2. Geriatric Clinic
Line 3. 3795 Paerdegat St.
Line 4. Loudonville, New York 11358

GROUP IV
Richmend General Hospital
Geriatric Clinic
3975 Paerdegat St.
Loudonville, New York 11538

11. In how many groups is line one exactly the same?   11.____

   A. Two   B. Three   C. Four   D. None

12. In how many groups is line two exactly the same?   12.____

   A. Two   B. Three   C. Four   D. None

13. In how many groups is line three exactly the same?   13.____

   A. Two   B. Three   C. Four   D. None

14. In how many groups is line four exactly the same? 14.___

   A. Two   B. Three   C. Four   D. None

Questions 15-18.

DIRECTIONS: Each of Questions 15 through 18 has two lists of names and addresses. Each list contains three sets of names and addresses. Check each of the three sets in the list on the right to see if they are the same as the corresponding set in the list on the left. Mark your answers:
- A. if none of the sets in the right list are the same as those in the left list
- B. if only one of the sets in the right list is the same as those in the left list
- C. if only two of the sets in the right list are the same as those in the left list
- D. if all three sets in the right list are the same as those in the left list

15.
Mary T. Berlinger
2351 Hampton St.
Monsey, N.Y. 20117

Eduardo Benes
473 Kingston Avenue
Central Islip, N.Y. 11734

Alan Carrington Fuchs
17 Gnarled Hollow Road
Los Angeles, CA 91635

Mary T. Berlinger
2351 Hampton St.
Monsey, N.Y. 20117

Eduardo Benes
473 Kingston Avenue
Central Islip, N.Y. 11734

Alan Carrington Fuchs
17 Gnarled Hollow Road
Los Angeles, CA 91685

15.___

16.
David John Jacobson
178 35 St. Apt. 4C
New York, N.Y. 00927

Ann-Marie Calonella
7243 South Ridge Blvd.
Bakersfield, CA 96714

Pauline M. Thompson
872 Linden Ave.
Houston, Texas 70321

David John Jacobson
178 53 St. Apt. 4C
New York, N.Y. 00927

Ann-Marie Calonella
7243 South Ridge Blvd.
Bakersfield, CA 96714

Pauline M. Thomson
872 Linden Ave.
Houston, Texas 70321

16.___

17.
Chester LeRoy Masterton
152 Lacy Rd.
Kankakee, Ill. 54532

William Maloney
S. LaCrosse Pla.
Wausau, Wisconsin 52146

Cynthia V. Barnes
16 Pines Rd.
Greenpoint, Miss. 20376

Chester LeRoy Masterson
152 Lacy Rd.
Kankakee, Ill. 54532

William Maloney
S. LaCross Pla.
Wausau, Wisconsin 52146

Cynthia V. Barnes
16 Pines Rd.
Greenpoint, Miss. 20376

17.___

18.

Marcel Jean Frontenac
8 Burton On The Water
Calender, Me. 01471

Marcel Jean Frontenac
6 Burton On The Water
Calender, Me. 01471

18.____

J. Scott Marsden
174 S. Tipton St.
Cleveland, Ohio

J. Scott Marsden
174 Tipton St.
Cleveland, Ohio

Lawrence T. Haney
171 McDonough St.
Decatur, Ga. 31304

Lawrence T. Haney
171 McDonough St.
Decatur, Ga. 31304

Questions 19-26.

DIRECTIONS: Each of Questions 19 through 26 has two lists of numbers. Each list contains three sets of numbers. Check each of the three sets in the list on the right to see if they are the same as the corresponding set in the list on the left. Mark your answers:
- A. if none of the sets in the right list are the same as those in the left list
- B. if only one of the sets in the right list is the same as those in the left list
- C. if only two of the sets in the right list are the same as those in the left list
- D. if all three sets in the right list are the same as those in the left list

19. 7354183476
4474747744
57914302311

7354983476
4474747774
57914302311

19.____

20. 7143592185
8344517699
9178531263

7143892185
8344518699
9178531263

20.____

21. 2572114731
8806835476
8255831246

257214731
8806835476
8255831246

21.____

22. 331476853821
6976658532996
3766042113715

331476858621
6976655832996
3766042113745

22.____

23. 8806663315
74477138449
211756663666

8806663315
74477138449
211756663666

23.____

24. 990006966996
53022219743
4171171117717

99000696996
53022219843
4171171177717

24.____

25. 24400222433004
5300030055000355
20000075532002022

24400222433004
5300030055500355
20000075532002022

25.____

26. 611166640660001116
     7111300117001100733
     26666446664476518

611166664066001116
7111300117001100733
26666446664476518

26.____

Questions 27-30.

DIRECTIONS: Questions 27 through 30 are to be answered by picking the answer which is in the correct numerical order, from the lowest number to the highest number, in each question.

27. A. 44533, 44518, 44516, 44547
     B. 44516, 44518, 44533, 44547
     C. 44547, 44533, 44518, 44516
     D. 44518, 44516, 44547, 44533

27.____

28. A. 95587, 95593, 95601, 95620
     B. 95601, 95620, 95587, 95593
     C. 95593, 95587, 95601, 95620
     D. 95620, 95601, 95593, 95587

28.____

29. A. 232212, 232208, 232232, 232223
     B. 232208, 232223, 232212, 232232
     C. 232208, 232212, 232223, 232232
     D. 232223, 232232, 232208, 232212

29.____

30. A. 113419, 113521, 113462, 113588
     B. 113588, 113462, 113521, 113419
     C. 113521, 113588, 113419, 113462
     D. 113419, 113462, 113521, 113588

30.____

KEY (CORRECT ANSWERS)

1.	C	11.	A	21.	C
2.	B	12.	C	22.	A
3.	D	13.	A	23.	D
4.	A	14.	A	24.	A
5.	C	15.	C	25.	C
6.	B	16.	B	26.	C
7.	D	17.	B	27.	B
8.	A	18.	B	28.	A
9.	D	19.	B	29.	C
10.	C	20.	B	30.	D

NAME AND NUMBER CHECKING

EXAMINATION SECTION
TEST 1

DIRECTIONS: Questions 1 through 17 consist of sets of names and addresses. In each question, the name and address in Column II should be an exact copy of the name and address in Column I.

If there is:
a mistake only in the name, mark your answer A;
a mistake only in the address, mark your answer B;
a mistake in both name and address, mark your answer C;
NO mistake in either name or address, mark your answer D.

SAMPLE QUESTION

Column I

Christina Magnusson
288 Greene Street
New York, N.Y. 10003

Column II

Christina Magnusson
288 Greene Street
New York, N.Y. 10013

Since there is a mistake only in the address (the zip code should be 10003 instead of 10013), the answer to the sample question is B.

COLUMN I	COLUMN II	
1. Ms. Joan Kelly 313 Franklin Ave. Brooklyn, N.Y. 11202	Ms. Joan Kielly 318 Franklin Ave. Brooklyn, N.Y. 11202	1.____
2. Mrs. Eileen Engel 47-24 86 Road Queens, N.Y. 11122	Mrs. Ellen Engel 47-24 86 Road Queens, N.Y. 11122	2.____
3. Marcia Michaels 213 E. 81 St. New York, N.Y. 10012	Marcia Michaels 213 E. 81 St. New York, N.Y. 10012	3.____
4. Rev. Edward J. Smyth 1401 Brandeis Street San Francisco, Calif. 96201	Rev. Edward J. Smyth 1401 Brandies Street San Francisco, Calif. 96201	4.____
5. Alicia Rodriguez 24-68 81 St. Elmhurst, N.Y. 11122	Alicia Rodriguez 2468 81 St. Elmhurst, N.Y. 11122	5.____
6. Ernest Eisemann 21 Columbia St. New York, N.Y. 10007	Ernest Eisermann 21 Columbia St. New York, N.Y. 10007	6.____

Column I	COLUMN II	
7. Mr. & Mrs. George Petersson 87-11 91st Avenue Woodhaven, N.Y. 11421	Mr. & Mrs. George Peterson 87-11 91st Avenue Woodhaven, N.Y. 11421	7._____
8. Mr. Ivan Klebnikov 1848 Newkirk Avenue Brooklyn, N.Y. 11226	Mr. Ivan Klebikov 1848 Newkirk Avenue Brooklyn, N.Y. 11622	8._____
9. Samuel Rothfleisch 71 Pine Street New York, N.Y. 10005	Samuel Rothfleisch 71 Pine Street New York, N.Y. 10005	9._____
10. Mrs. Isabel Tonnessen 198 East 185th Street Bronx, N.Y. 10458	Mrs. Isabel Tonnessen 189 East 185th Street Bronx, N.Y. 10458	10._____
11. Esteban Perez 173 Eighth Street Staten Island, N.Y. 10306	Estaban Perez 173 Eighth Street Staten Island, N.Y. 10306	11._____
12. Esta Wong 141 West 68 St. New York, N.Y. 10023	Esta Wang 141 West 68 St. New York, N.Y. 10023	12._____
13. Dr. Alberto Grosso 3475 12th Avenue Brooklyn, N.Y. 11218	Dr. Alberto Grosso 3475 12th Avenue Brooklyn, N.Y. 11218	13._____
14. Mrs. Ruth Bortlas 482 Theresa Ct. Far Rockaway, N.Y. 11691	Ms. Ruth Bortlas 482 Theresa Ct. Far Rockaway, N.Y. 11169	14._____
15. Mr. & Mrs. Howard Fox 2301 Sedgwick Ave. Bronx, N.Y. 10468	Mr. & Mrs. Howard Fox 231 Sedgwick Ave. Bronx, N.Y. 10468	15._____
16. Miss Marjorie Black 223 East 23 Street New York, N.Y. 10010	Miss Margorie Black 223 East 23 Street New York, N.Y. 10010	16._____
17. Michelle Herman 806 Valley Rd. Old Tappan, N.J. 07675	Michelle Hermann 806 Valley Dr. Old Tappan, N.J. 07675	17._____

———————

KEY (CORRECT ANSWERS)

1.	C		6.	A
2.	A		7.	A
3.	D		8.	C
4.	B		9.	D
5.	B		10.	B

11.	A
12.	A
13.	D
14.	C
15.	B
16.	A
17.	C

———

TEST 2

DIRECTIONS: Questions 1 through 15 are to be answered SOLELY on the instructions given below. *PRINT THE LETTER OF THE CORRECT ANSWER IN THE SPACE AT THE RIGHT.*

INSTRUCTIONS:

In each of the following questions, the 3-line name and address in Column I is the master-list entry, and the 3-line entry in Column 2 is the information to be checked against the master list. If there is one line that does not match, mark your answer A; if there are two lines that do not match, mark your answer B; if all three lines do not match, mark your answer C; if the lines all match exactly, mark your answer D.

SAMPLE QUESTION

Column I
Mark L. Field
11-09 Prince Park Blvd.
Bronx, N.Y. 11402

Column II
Mark L. Field
11-99 Prince Park Way
Bronx, N.Y. 11401

The first lines in each column match exactly. The second lines do not match since 11-09 does not match 11-99; and Blvd. does not match Way. The third lines do not match either since 11402 does not match 11401. Therefore, there are two lines that do not match, and the CORRECT answer is B.

COLUMN I	COLUMN II	
1. Jerome A. Jackson 1243 14th Avenue New York, N.Y. 10023	Jerome A. Johnson 1234 14th Avenue New York, N.Y. 10023	1.__
2. Sophie Strachtheim 33-28 Connecticut Ave. Far Rockaway, N.Y. 11697	Sophie Strachtheim 33-28 Connecticut Ave. Far Rockaway, N.Y. 11697	2.__
3. Elisabeth N.T. Gorrell 256 Exchange St. New York, N.Y. 10013	Elizabeth N.T. Gorrell 256 Exchange St. New York, N.Y. 10013	3.__
4. Maria J. Gonzalez 7516 E. Sheepshead Rd. Brooklyn, N.Y. 11240	Maria J. Gonzalez 7516 N. Shepshead Rd. Brooklyn, N.Y. 11240	4.__
5. Leslie B. Brautenweiler 21 57A Seiler Terr. Flushing, N.Y. 11367	Leslie B. Brautenwieler 21-75A Seiler Terr. Flushing, N.J. 11367	5.__
6. Rigoberto J. Peredes 157 Twin Towers, #18F Tottenville, S.I., N.Y.	Rigoberto J. Peredes 157 Twin Towers, #18F Tottenville, S.I., N.Y.	6.__

COLUMN I	COLUMN II	
7. Pietro F. Albino P.O. Box 7548 Floral Park, N.Y. 11005	Pietro F. Albina P.O. Box 7458 Floral Park, N.Y. 11005	7._____
8. Joanne Zimmermann Bldg. SW, Room 314 532-4601	Joanne Zimmermann Bldg. SW, Room 314 532-4601	8._____
9. Carlyle Whetstone Payroll Div.-A, Room 212A 262-5000, ext. 471	Caryle Whetstone Payroll Div.-A, Room 212A 262-5000, ext. 417	9._____
10. Kenneth Chiang Legal Council, Room 9745 (201) 416-9100, ext. 17	Kenneth Chiang Legal Counsel, Room 9745 (201) 416-9100, ext. 17	10._____
11. Ethel Koenig Personnel Services Division, Room 433; 635-7572	Ethel Hoenig Personal Services Division, Room 433; 635-7527	11._____
12. Joyce Ehrhardt Office of the Administrator, Room W56; 387-8706	Joyce Ehrhart Office of the Administrator, Room W56; 387-7806	12._____
13. Ruth Lang EAM Bldg., Room C101 625-2000, ext. 765	Ruth Lang EAM Bldg., Room C110 625-2000, ext. 765	13._____
14. Anne Marie Ionozzi Investigations, Room 827 576-4000, ext. 832	Anna Marie Ionozzi Investigation, Room 827 566-4000, ext. 832	14._____
15. Willard Jameson Fm C Bldg., Room 687 454-3010	Willard Jamieson Fm C Bldg., Room 687 454-3010	15._____

KEY (CORRECT ANSWERS)

1.	B	6.	D
2.	D	7.	B
3.	A	8.	D
4.	A	9.	B
5.	C	10.	A

11.	C
12.	B
13.	A
14.	C
15.	A

TEST 3

DIRECTIONS: Questions 1 through 10 are to be answered on the basis of the following instructions. *PRINT THE LETTER OF THE CORRECT ANSWER IN THE SPACE AT THE RIGHT.*

INSTRUCTIONS:

For each such set of names, addresses, and numbers listed in Columns I and II, select your answer from the following options:

A. The names in Columns I and II are different.
B. The addresses in Columns I and II are different.
C. The numbers in Columns I and II are different.
D. The names, addresses, and numbers in Columns I and II are identical.

COLUMN I   COLUMN II

1. Francis Jones   Francis Jones   1.____
   62 Stately Avenue   62 Stately Avenue
   96-12446   96-21446

2. Julio Montez   Julio Montez   2.____
   19 Ponderosa Road   19 Ponderosa Road
   56-73161   56-71361

3. Mary Mitchell   Mary Mitchell   3.____
   2314 Melbourne Drive   2314 Melbourne Drive
   68-92172   68-92172

4. Harry Patterson   Harry Patterson   4.____
   25 Dunne Street   25 Dunne Street
   14-33430   14-34330

5. Patrick Murphy   Patrick Murphy   5.____
   171 West Hosmer Street   171 West Hosmer Street
   93-81214   93-18214

6. August Schultz   August Schultz   6.____
   816 St. Clair Avenue   816 St. Claire Avenue
   53-40149   53-40149

7. George Taft   George Taft   7.____
   72 Runnymede Street   72 Runnymede Street
   47-04033   47-04023

8. Angus Henderson   Angus Henderson   8.____
   1418 Madison Street   1418 Madison Street
   81-76375   81-76375

9. Carolyn Mazur   Carolyn Mazur   9.____
   12 Riverview Road   12 Rivervane ftoad
   38-99615   38-99615

COLUMN I

10. Adele Russell
1725 Lansing Lane
72-91962

COLUMN II

Adela Russell
1725 Lansing Lane
72-91962

10.____

_____

KEY (CORRECT ANSWERS)

1. C
2. C
3. D
4. C
5. C

6. B
7. C
8. D
9. B
10. A

_____

TEST 4

DIRECTIONS: Questions 1 through 20 test how good you are at catching mistakes in typing or printing. In each question, the name and address in Column II should be an exact copy of the name and address in Column I. Mark your answer

- A. if there is no mistake in either name or address;
- B. if there is a mistake in both name and address;
- C. if there is a mistake only in the name;
- D. if there is a mistake only in the address.

PRINT THE LETTER OF THE CORRECT ANSWER IN THE SPACE AT THE RIGHT.

COLUMN I   COLUMN II

1. Milos Yanocek   Milos Yanocek   1._____
    33-60 14 Street   33-60 14 Street
    Long Island City, N.Y. 11011   Long Island City, N.Y. 11001

2. Alphonse Sabattelo   Alphonse Sabbattelo   2._____
    24 Minnetta Lane   24 Minetta Lane
    New York, N.Y. 10006   New York, N.Y. 10006

3. Helen Steam   Helene Stearn   3._____
    5 Metropolitan Oval   5 Metropolitan Oval
    Bronx, N.Y. 10462   Bronx, N.Y. 10462

4. Jacob Weisman   Jacob Weisman   4._____
    231 Francis Lewis Boulevard   231 Francis Lewis Boulevard
    Forest Hills, N.Y. 11325   Forest Hills, N.Y. 11325

5. Riccardo Fuente   Riccardo Fuentes   5._____
    134 West 83 Street   134 West 88 Street
    New York, N.Y. 10024   New York, N.Y. 10024

6. Dennis Lauber   Dennis Lauder   6._____
    52 Avenue D   52 Avenue D
    Brooklyn, N.Y. 11216   Brooklyn, N.Y. 11216

7. Paul Cutter   Paul Cutter   7._____
    195 Galloway Avenue   175 Galloway Avenue
    Staten Island, N.Y. 10356   Staten Island, N.Y. 10365

8. Sean Donnelly   Sean Donnelly   8._____
    45-58 41 Avenue   45-58 41 Avenue
    Woodside, N.Y. 11168   Woodside, N.Y. 11168

9. Clyde Willot   Clyde Willat   9._____
    1483 Rockaway Avenue   1483 Rockway Avenue
    Brooklyn, N.Y. 11238   Brooklyn, N.Y. 11238

COLUMN I	COLUMN II	
10. Michael Stanakis 419 Sheriden Avenue Staten Island, N.Y. 10363	Michael Stanakis 419 Sheraden Avenue Staten Island, N.Y. 10363	10.____
11. Joseph DiSilva 63-84 Saunders Road Rego Park, N.Y. 11431	Joseph Disilva 64-83 Saunders Road Rego Park, N.Y. 11431	11.____
12. Linda Polansky 2225 Fenton Avenue Bronx, N.Y. 10464	Linda Polansky 2255 Fenton Avenue Bronx, N.Y. 10464	12.____
13. Alfred Klein 260 Hillside Terrace Staten Island, N.Y. 15545	Alfred Klein 260 Hillside Terrace Staten Island, N.Y. 15545	13.____
14. William McDonnell 504 E. 55 Street New York, N.Y. 10103	William McConnell 504 E. 55 Street New York, N.Y. 10108	14.____
15. Angela Cipolla 41-11 Parson Avenue Flushing, N.Y. 11446	Angela Cipola 41-11 Parsons Avenue Flushing, N.Y. 11446	15.____
16. Julie Sheridan 1212 Ocean Avenue Brooklyn, N.Y. 11237	Julia Sheridan 1212 Ocean Avenue Brooklyn, N.Y. 11237	16.____
17. Arturo Rodriguez 2156 Cruger Avenue Bronx, N.Y. 10446	Arturo Rodrigues 2156 Cruger Avenue Bronx, N.Y. 10446	17.____
18. Helen McCabe 2044 East 19 Street Brooklyn, N.Y. 11204	Helen McCabe 2040 East 19 Street Brooklyn,. N.Y. 11204	18.____
19. Charles Martin 526 West 160 Street New York, N.Y. 10022	Charles Martin 526 West 160 Street New York, N.Y. 10022	19.____
20. Morris Rabinowitz 31 Avenue M Brooklyn, N.Y. 11216	Morris Rabinowitz 31 Avenue N Brooklyn, N.Y. 11216	20.____

KEY (CORRECT ANSWERS)

1.	D		11.	B
2.	B		12.	D
3.	C		13.	A
4.	A		14.	B
5.	B		15.	B
6.	C		16.	C
7.	D		17.	C
8.	A		18.	D
9.	B		19.	A
10.	D		20.	D

———

TEST 5

DIRECTIONS: In copying the addresses below from Column A to the same line in Column B, an Agent-in-Training made some errors. For Questions 1 through 5, if you find that the Agent made an error in

only one line, mark your answer A;
only two lines, mark your answer B;
only three lines, mark your answer C;
all four lines, mark your answer D.

EXAMPLE

Column A

24 Third Avenue
5 Lincoln Road
50 Central Park West
37-21 Queens Boulevard

Column B

24 Third Avenue
5 Lincoln Street
6 Central Park West
21-37 Queens Boulevard

Since errors were made on only three lines, namely the second, third, and fourth, the CORRECT answer is C.
PRINT THE LETTER OF THE CORRECT ANSWER IN THE SPACE AT THE RIGHT.

Column A

Column B

1. 57-22 Springfield Boulevard
    94 Gun Hill Road
    8 New Dorp Lane
    36 Bedford Avenue

    75-22 Springfield Boulevard
    94 Gun Hill Avenue
    8 New Drop Lane
    36 Bedford Avenue   1.___

2. 538 Castle Hill Avenue
    54-15 Beach Channel Drive
    21 Ralph Avenue
    162 Madison Avenue

    538 Castle Hill Avenue
    54-15 Beach Channel Drive
    21 Ralph Avenue
    162 Morrison Avenue   2.___

3. 49 Thomas Street
    27-21 Northern Blvd.
    86 125th Street
    872 Atlantic Ave.

    49 Thomas Street
    21-27 Northern Blvd.
    86 125th Street
    872 Baltic Ave.   3.___

4. 261-17 Horace Harding Expwy.
    191 Fordham Road
    6 Victory Blvd.
    552 Oceanic Ave.

    261-17 Horace Harding Pkwy.
    191 Fordham Road
    6 Victoria Blvd.
    552 Ocean Ave.   4.___

5. 90-05 38th Avenue
    19 Central Park West
    9281 Avenue X
    22 West Farms Square

    90-05 36th Avenue
    19 Central Park East
    9281 Avenue X
    22 West Farms Square   5.___

KEY (CORRECT ANSWERS)

1. C
2. A
3. B
4. C
5. B

_____

TEST 6

Questions 1-10.

DIRECTIONS: For Questions 1 through 10, choose the letter in Column II next to the number which EXACTLY matches the number in Column I. *PRINT THE LETTER OF THE CORRECT ANSWER IN THE SPACE AT THE RIGHT.*

<u>COLUMN I</u>   <u>COLUMN II</u>

1. 14235
                                        A. 13254
                                        B. 12435
                                        C. 13245
                                        D. 14235   1._____

2. 70698
    A. 90768
    B. 60978
    C. 70698
    D. 70968   2._____

3. 11698
    A. 11689
    B. 11986
    C. 11968
    D. 11698   3._____

4. 50497
    A. 50947
    B. 50497
    C. 50749
    D. 54097   4._____

5. 69635
    A. 60653
    B. 69630
    C. 69365
    D. 69635   5._____

6. 1201022011
    A. 1201022011
    B. 1201020211
    C. 1202012011
    D. 1021202011   6._____

7. 3893981389
    A. 3893891389
    B. 3983981389
    C. 3983891389
    D. 3893981389   7._____

8. 4765476589
    A. 4765476598
    B. 4765476588
    C. 4765476589
    D. 4765746589   8._____

COLUMN I	COLUMN II	
9. 8679678938	A. 8679687938 B. 8679678938 C. 8697678938 D. 8678678938	9.____
10. 6834836932	A. 6834386932 B. 6834836923 C. 6843836932 D. 6834836932	10.____

Questions 11-15.

DIRECTIONS: For Questions 11 through 15, determine how many of the symbols in Column Z are exactly the same as the symbol in Column Y.
If none is exactly the same, answer A;
if only one symbol is exactly the same, answer B;
if two symbols are exactly the same, answer C;
if three symbols are exactly the same, answer D.

COLUMN Y	COLUMN Z	
11. A123B1266	A123B1366 A123B1266 A133B1366 A123B1266	11.____
12. CC28D3377	CD22D3377 CC38D3377 CC28C3377 CC28D2277	12.____
13. M21AB201X	M12AB201X M21AB201X M21AB201Y M21BA201X	13.____
14. PA383Y744	AP383Y744 PA338Y744 PA388Y744 PA383Y774	14.____
15. PB2Y8893	PB2Y8893 PB2Y8893 PB3Y8898 PB2Y8893	15.____

KEY (CORRECT ANSWERS)

1.	D		6.	A
2.	C		7.	D
3.	D		8.	C
4.	B		9.	B
5.	D		10.	D

11.	C
12.	A
13.	B
14.	A
15.	D

FILING

EXAMINATION SECTION
TEST 1

Question 1-9

DIRECTIONS: An important part of the duties of an office worker in a public agency is to file office records. Questions 1 to 9 are designed to determine whether you can file records correctly. Each of these questions consists of four names. For each question, select the one of the four names that should be *FOURTH* if the four names were arranged in alphabetical order. *PRINT THE LETTER OF THE CORRECT ANSWER IN THE SPACE AT THE RIGHT.*

1. A. 6th National Bank   B. Sexton Lock Co.   1.____
    C. The 69th Street League   D. Thomas Saxon Corp,

2. A. 4th Avenue Printing Co.   B. The Four Corners Corp.   2.____
    C. Dr. Milton Fournet   D. The Martin Fountaine Co.

3. A. Mr. Chas. Le Mond   B. Model Express, Inc.   3.____
    C. Lenox Enterprises   D. Mobile Supply Co.

4. A. Frank Waller Johnson   B. Frank Walter Johnson   4.____
    C. Wilson Johnson   D. Frank W. Johnson

5. A. Miss Anne M. Carlsen   B. Mrs, Albert S. Carlson   5.____
    C. Mr. Alan Ross Carlsen   D. Dr. Anthony Ash Carlson

6. A. Delware Paper Co.   B. William Del Ville   6.____
    C. Ralph A. Delmar   D. Wm. K. Del Ville

7. A. The Lloyd Disney Co.   B. Mrs. Raymond Norris   7.____
    C. Oklahoma Envelope, Inc.   D. Miss Esther O'Neill

8. A. The Olympic Eraser Co.   B. Mrs. Raymond Norris   8.____
    C. Oklahoma Envelope, Inc.   D. Miss Esther O'Neill

9. A. Patricia MacNamara   B. Eleanor McNally   9.____
    C. Robt. MacPherson, Jr.   D. Helen McNair

Questions 10 - 21

DIRECTIONS: Questions 10 through 21 are to be answered on the basis of the usual rules for alphabetical filing. For each question, indicate in the space at the right the letter preceding the name which should be *THIRD* in alphabetical order.

10. A. Russell Cohen   B. Henry Cohn   10.____
    C. Wesley Chambers   D. Arthur Connors

11. A. Wanda Jenkins   B. Pauline Jennings   11.____
    C. Leslie Jantzenberg   D. Rudy Jensen

12. A. Arnold Wilson   B. Carlton Willson   12.____
    C. Duncan Williamson   D. Ezra Wilston

13. A. Joseph M. Buchman   B. Gustave Bozzerman   13.____
     C. Constantino Brunelli   D. Armando Buccino

14. A. Barbara Waverly   B. Corinne Warterdam   14.____
     C. Dennis Waterman   D. Harold Wartman

15. A. Jose Mejia   B. Bernard Mendelsohn   15.____
     C. Antonio Mejias   D. Richard Mazzitelli

16. A. Hesselberg, Norman J.   B. Hesselman, Nathan B.   16.____
     C. Hazel, Robert S.   D. Heintz, August J.

17. A. Oshins, Jerome   B. Ohsie, Marjorie   17.____
     C. O'Shaugn, F.J.   D. O'Shea, Frances

18. A. Petrie, Joshua A.   B. Pendleton, Oscar   18.____
     C. Pertwee, Joshua   D. Perkins, Warren G.

19. A. Morganstern, Alfred   B. Morganstern, Albert   19.____
     C. Monroe, Mildred   D. Modesti, Ernest

20. A. More, Stewart   B. Moorhead, Jay   20.____
     C. Moore, Benjamin   D. Moffat, Edith

21. A. Ramirez, Paul   B. Revere, Pauline   21.____
     C. Ramos, Felix   D. Ramazotti, Angelo

KEY (CORRECT ANSWERS)

1.	C	11.	B
2.	A	12.	A
3.	B	13.	D
4.	B	14.	C
5.	D	15.	C
6.	A	16.	A
7.	C	17.	D
8.	D	18.	C
9.	B	19.	B
10.	B	20.	B

21. C

TEST 2

DIRECTIONS: Each question or incomplete statement is followed by several suggested answers or completions. Select the one that *BEST* answers the question or completes the statement. *PRINT THE LETTER OF THE CORRECT ANSWER IN THE SPACE AT THE RIGHT.*

Questions 1 - 4

DIRECTIONS: Answer Questions 1 through 4 on the basis of the following alphabetical rules.

RULES FOR ALPHABETICAL FILING

Names of Individuals

The names of individuals are filed in strict alphabetical order, *first* according to the last name, *then* according to first name or initial, and *finally* according to middle name or initial. For example: George Allen precedes Edward Bell and Leonard Reston precedes Lucille Reston.

When last names are the same, for example, A. Green and Agnes Green, the one with the initial comes before the one with the name written out when the first initials are identical,

Prefixes such as De, O', Mac, Mc, and Van are filed as written and are treated as part of the names to which they are connected. For example: Gladys McTeaque is filed before Frances Meadows.

1. If the following four names were put into an alphabetical list, what would the *FIRST* name on the list be?
    1._____

    A. Wm. C. Paul   B. W. Paul
    C. Alice Paul   D. Alyce Paule

2. If the following four names were put into an alphabetical list *what* would the *THIRD* name on the list be?
    2._____

    A. I. MacCarthy   B. Irene MacKarthy
    C. Ida McCaren   D. I. A. McCarthy

3. If the following four names were put into an alphabetical list, *what* would the *SECOND* name on the list be?
    3._____

    A. John Gilhooley   B. Ramon Gonzalez
    C. Gerald Gilholy   D. Samuel Gilvecchio

4. If the following four names were put into an alphabetical list, *what,* would the *FOURTH* name on the list be?
    4._____

    A. Michael Edwinn   B. James Edwards
    C. Mary Edwin   D. Carlo Edwards

Questions 5-9

DIRECTIONS: Questions 5 to 9 consist of a group of names which are to be arranged in alphabetical order for filing.

5. Of the following, the name which should be filed *FIRST* is   5.____

    A. Joseph J. Meadeen   B. Gerard L. Meader
    C. John F. Madcar   D. Philip F. Malder

6. Of the following, the name which should be filed *LAST* is   6.____

    A. Stephen Fischer   B. Benjamin Fitchmann
    C. Thomas Fishman   D. Augustus S. Fisher

7. The name which should be filed *SECOND* is   7.____

    A. Yeatman, Frances   B. Yeaton, C.S.
    C. Yeatman, R.M.   D. Yeats, John

8. The name which should be filed *THIRD* is   8.____

    A. Hauser, Ann   B. Hauptmann, Jane
    C. Hauster, Mary   D. Rauprich, Julia

9. The name which should be filed *SECOND* is   9.____

    A. Flora McDougall   B. Fred E. MacDowell
    C. Juanita Mendez   D. James A. Madden

Questions 10-14

DIRECTIONS: Answer questions 10 through 14 based on an alphabetical arrangement of the following list of names.

Walker, Carol J.	Wacht, Michael	Wade, Ethel
Wall, Fredrick	Wall, Francis	Wall, Frank
Wachs, Paul	Walker, Carol L.	Wagner, Arthur
Walters, Daniel	Wade, Ellen	Wald, William
Wagner, Allen	Walters, David	Walker, Carmen

10. The 4th name on the alphabetized list would be   10.____

    A. Wade,Ellen   B. Wade, Ethel
    C. Wagner, Allen   D. Wagner, Arthur

11. The 7th name on the alphabetized list would be   11.____

    A. Walker, Carmen   B. Walker, Carol J.
    C. Walker, Carol L.   D. Wald, William

12. The name that would come immediately AFTER Wagner, Arthur on the alphabetized list would be   12.____

    A. Wade, Ethel   B. Wagner, Allen
    C. Wald, William   D. Walker, Carol L.

13. The name that would come immediately BEFORE Wall, Frank would be   13.____

    A. Wall, Francis   B. Wall, Fredrick
    C. Walters, David   D. Walters, Daniel

14.   The 12th name on the alphabetized list would be   14.____

   A.   Walker, Carol L.   B.   Wald, William
   C.   Wall, Francis   D.   Wall, Frank

_____

KEY (CORRECT ANSWERS)

   1.   C   6.   B
   2.   C   7.   C
   3.   A   8.   A
   4.   A   9.   D
   5.   C   10.   B

         11.   D
         12.   C
         13.   A
         14.   D

_____

TEST 3

DIRECTIONS: Each question or incomplete statement is followed by several suggested answers or completions. Select the one that *BEST* answers the question or completes the statement. *PRINT THE LETTER OF THE CORRECT ANSWER IN THE SPACE AT THE RIGHT.*

Questions 1-8

DIRECTIONS: Questions 1 through 8 are based on the Rules of Alphabetical Filing given below. Read these rules carefully before answering the questions.

Names of People

1. The names of people are filed in strict alphabetical order, first according to the last name, then according to first name or initial, and finally according to middle name or initial. For example: George Allen comes before Edward Bell, and Leonard P. Reston comes before Lucille B. Reston.

2. When last names are the same, for example, A. Green and Agnes Green, the one with the initial comes before the one with the name written out when the first initials are identical.

3. When first and last names are alike and the middle name is given, for example, John David Doe and John Devoe Doe, the names should be filed in alphabetical order of the middle names.

4. When first and last names are the same, a name without a middle initial comes before one with a middle name or initial. For example: John Doe comes before John A. Doe and John Alan Doe.

5. When first and last names are the same, a name with a middle initial comes before one with a middle name beginning with the same initial. For example: Jack R. Hertz comes before Jack Richard Hertz.

6. Prefixes such De, O', Mac, Mc and Van are filed as written and are treated as part of the names to which they are connected. For example: Robert O'Dea is filed before David Olsen.

7. Abbreviated names are treated as if they were spelled out. For example: Chas. is filed as Charles and Thos. is filed as Thomas.

8. Titles and designations such as Dr., Mr., and Prof, are disregarded in filing.

Names of Organizations

1. The names of business organizations are filed according to the order in which each word in the name appears. When an organization name bears the name of a person, it is filed according to the rules for filing names of people as given above. For example: William Smith Service Co. comes before Television Distributors, Inc.

2. Where bureau, board, office or department appears as the first part of the title of a governmental agency, that agency should be filed under the word in the title expressing the chief function of the agency. For example: Bureau of Budget would be filed as if written Budget, (Bureau of the). The Department of Personnel would be filed as if written Personnel, (Department of).

3. When the following words are part of an organization, they are disregarded: the, of, and.

4. When there are numbers in a name, they are treated as if they were spelled out. For example: 10th Street Bootery is filed as Tenth Street Bootery.

Each question from 1 through 8 contains four names numbered from 1 through 4 but not necessarily numbered in correct filing order. Answer each question by choosing the letter corresponding to the *CORRECT* filing order of the four names in accordance with the above rules.

Sample question:

    1. Robert J. Smith
    2. R. Jeffrey Smith
    3. Dr. A. Smythe
    4. Allen R. Smithers

A. 1, 2, 3, 4   B. 3, 1, 2, 4   C. 2, 1, 4, 3   D. 3, 2, 1, 4

Since the correct filing order, in accordance with the above rules, is 2, 1, 4, 3, the correct answer is C.

1. 1. J. Chester VanClief   2. John C. VanClief   1.____
    3. J. VanCleve   4. Mary L. Vance

    A. 4, 3, 1, 2   B. 4, 3, 2, 1   C. 3, 1, 2, 4   D. 3, 4, 1, 2

2. 1. Community Development Agency   2.____
    2. Department of Social Services
    3. Board of Estimate
    4. Bureau of Gas and Electricity

    A. 3, 4, 1, 2   B. 1, 2, 4, 3   C. 2, 1, 3, 4   D. 1, 3, 4, 2

3. 1. Dr. Chas. K. Dahlman   3.____
    2. F. & A. Delivery Service
    3. Department of Water Supply
    4. Demano Men's Custom Tailors

    A. 1, 2, 3, 4   B. 1, 4, 2, 3   C. 4, 1, 2, 3   D. 4, 1, 3, 2

4. 1. 48th Street Theater   4.____
    2. Fourteenth Street Day Care Center
    3. Professor A. Cartwright
    4. Albert F. McCarthy

    A. 4, 2, 1, 3   B. 4, 3, 1, 2   C. 3, 2, 1, 4   D. 3, 1, 2, 4

5.　1.　Frances D'Arcy　　　　2.　Mario L. DelAmato　　　　　5.___
　　3.　William R. Diamond　　4.　Robert J. DuBarry

　　A.　1, 2, 4, 3　　　B.　2, 1, 3, 4　　　C.　1, 2, 3, 4　　　D.　2, 1, 3, 4

6.　1.　Evelyn H. D'Amelio　　2.　Jane R. Bailey　　　　　　6.___
　　3.　Robert Bailey　　　　　4.　Frank Baily

　　A.　1, 2, 3, 4　　　B.　1, 3, 2, 4　　　C.　2, 3, 4, 1　　　D.　3, 2, 4, 1

7.　1.　Department of Markets　　　　　　　　　　　　　　　7.___
　　2.　Bureau of Handicapped Children
　　3.　Housing Authority Administration Building
　　4.　Board of Pharmacy

　　A.　2, 1, 3, 4　　　B.　1, 2, 4, 3　　　C.　1, 2, 3, 4　　　D.　3, 2, 1, 4

8.　1.　William A. Shea Stadium　　　　　　　　　　　　　　8.___
　　2.　Rapid Speed Taxi Co.
　　3.　Harry Stampler's Rotisserie
　　4.　Wilhelm Albert Shea

　　A.　2, 3, 4, 1　　　B.　4, 1, 3, 2　　　C.　2, 4, 1, 3　　　D.　3, 4, 1, 2

Questions 9-18.

DIRECTIONS:　Questions 9 through 18 each show in Column I names written on four ledger cards (lettered w, x, y, z) which have to be filed. You are to choose the option (lettered A, B, C, or D) in Column II which *BEST* represents the proper order for filing the cards.

SAMPLE

Column I		Column II	
w.	John Stevens	A.	w, y , z, x
x.	John D. Stevenson	B.	y, w, z, x
y.	Joan Stevens	C.	x, y, w, z
z.	J. Stevenson	D.	x, w, y, z

The correct way to file the cards is:
y. Joan Stevens
w. John Stevens
z. J. Stevenson
x. John D. Stevenson

The correct order is shown by the letters y, w, z, x in that sequence. Since, in Column II, B appears in front of the letters y, w, z, x in that sequence, B is the correct answer to the sample question.

Now, answer the following questions, using the same procedure.

	Column I		Column II	
9.	w.	Juan Montoya	A.	y, z, x, w
	x.	Manuel Montenegro	B.	z, y, x, w
	y.	Victor Matos	C.	z, y, w, x
	z.	Victoria Maltos	D.	y, x, z, w

10.	w. Frank Carlson	A. z, x, w, y
	x. Robert Carlton	B. z, y, x, w
	y. George Carlson	C. w, y, z, x
	z. Frank Carlton	D. w, z, y, x

11.	w. Carmine Rivera	A. y, w, x, z
	x. Jose Rivera	B. y, x, w, z
	y. Frank River	C. w, x, y, z
	z. Joan Rivers	D. w, x, z, y

12.	w. Jerome Mathews	A. w, y, z, x
	x. Scott A. Matthew	B. z, y, x, w
	y. Charles B. Matthew	C. z, w, x, y
	z. Scott C. Mathews	D. w, z, y, x

13.	w. John McMahan	A. w, x, y, z
	x. John P. MacMahan	B. y, x, z, w
	y. Joseph DeMayo	C. x, w, y, z
	z. Joseph D. Mayo	D. y, x, w, z

14.	w. Raymond Martinez	A. z, x, y, w
	x. Ramon Martinez	B. z, y, x, w
	y. Prof. Ray Martinez	C. z, w, y, x
	z. Dr. Raymond Martin	D. y, x, w, z

15.	w. Mr. Robert Vincent Mackintosh	A. y, x, z, w
	x. Robert Reginald Macintosh	B. x, w, z, y
	y. Roger V. McIntosh	C. x, w, y, z
	z. Robert R. Mackintosh	D. x, z, w, y

16.	w. Dr. D. V. Facsone	A. y, w, z, x
	x. Prof. David Fascone	B. w, y, x, z
	y. Donald Facsone	C. w, y, z, x
	z. Mrs. D. Fascone	D. z, w, x, y

17.	w. Johnathan Q. Addams	A. z, x, w, y
	x. John Quincy Adams	B. z, x, y, w
	y. J. Quincy Addams	C. y, w, x, z
	z. Jerimiah Adams	D. x, w, z, y

18.	w. Nehimiah Persoff	A. w, z, x, y
	x. Newton Pershing	B. x, z, y, w
	y. Newman Perring	C. y, x, w, z
	z. Nelson Persons	D. z, y, w, x

KEY (CORRECT ANSWERS)

1.	A		11.	A
2.	D		12.	D
3.	B		13.	B
4.	D		14.	A
5.	C		15.	D
6.	D		16.	C
7.	D		17.	B
8.	C		18.	C
9.	B			
10.	C			

———

TEST 4

Questions: 1 - 13

DIRECTIONS: Each question from 1 through 13 contains four names. For each question, choose the name that should be *FIRST* if the four names are to be arranged in alphabetical order in accordance with the Rule for Alphabetical Filing of Names of People given below. Read this rule carefully. Then, for each question, mark your answer space with the letter that is next to the name that should be first in alphabetical order.

RULE FOR ALPHABETICAL FILING OF NAMES OF PEOPLE

The names of people are filed in strict alphabetical order, first according to the last name, then according to the first name. For example: George Allen comes before Edward Bell, and Alice Reston comes before Lucille Reston.

SAMPLE QUESTION
A. Roger Smith (2)
B. Joan Smythe (4)
C. Alan Smith (1)
D. James Smithe(3)

The numbers in parentheses show the proper alphabetical order in which these names should be filed. Since the name that should be filed *first* is Alan Smith, the correct answer to the sample question is C.

1. A. William Claremont   B. Antonio Clements   1.____
    C. Anthony Clemente   D. William Claymont

2. A. Wayne Fumando   B. Sarah Femando   2.____
    C. Susan Fumando   D. Wilson Femando

3. A. Wilbur Hanson   B. Wm. Hansen   3.____
    C. Robert Hansen   D. Thomas Hanson

4. A. George St. John   B. Thomas Santos   4.____
    C. Frances Starks   D. Mary S. Stranum

5. A. Franklin Carrol   B. Timothy Carrol   5.____
    C. Timothy S. Carol   D. Frank F. Carroll

6. A. Christie-Barry Storage   B. John Christie-Barry   6.____
    C. The Christie-Barry Company D. Anne Christie-Barrie

7. A. Inter State Travel Co.   B. Interstate Car Rental   7.____
    C. Inter State Trucking   D. Interstate Lending Inst.

8. A. The Los Angeles Tile Co. B. Anita F. Los   8.____
    C. The Lost & Found Detective Agency D. Jason Los-Brio

9. A. Prince Charles   B. Prince Charles Coiffures 9.____
    C. Chas. F. Prince   D. Thomas A. Charles

10.   A. U.S. Dept. of Agriculture   B. United States Aircraft Co.   10.___
       C. U.S. Air Transport, Inc.   D. The United Union

11.   A. Meyer's Art Shop   B. Frank B. Meyer   11.___
       C. Meyers' Paint Store   D. Meyer and Goldberg

12.   A. David Des Laurier   B. Des Moines Flower Shop   12.___
       C. Henry Desanto   D. Mary L. Desta

13.   A. Jeffrey Van Der Meer   B. Jeffrey M. Vander   13.___
       C. Jeffrey Van   D. Wallace Meer

KEY (CORRECT ANSWERS)

1.	A		6.	D
2.	B		7.	B
3.	C		8.	B
4.	A		9.	D
5.	C		10.	C

11.	A
12.	C
13.	D

TEST 5

Questions: 1-10

DIRECTIONS: Questions 1 to 10 are to be answered on the basis of the usual rules of filing. Column I lists, next to the numbers 1 to 10, the names of 10 clinic patients. Column II lists, next to the letters A to D, the headings of file drawers into which you are to place the records of these patients. For each question, indicate in the space at the right the letter preceding the heading of the file drawer in which the record should be filed.

COLUMN I	COLUMN II	
1. Charles Coughlin	A. Cab-Cep	1.____
2. Mary Carstairs	B. Ceq-Cho	2.____
3. Joseph Collin	C. Chr-Coj	3.____
4. Thomas Chelsey	D. Cok-Czy	4.____
5. Cedric Chalmers		5.____
6. Mae Clarke		6.____
7. Dora Copperhead		7.____
8. Arnold Cohn		8.____
9. Charlotte Crumboldt		9.____
10. Frances Celine		10.____

Questions 11-18

DIRECTIONS: Questions 11 to 18 are to be answered on the basis of the usual rules of filing. Column I lists, next to the numbers 11 to 18, the names of 8 clinic patients. Column II lists, next to the letters A to O, the headings of file drawers into which you are to place the records of these patients. For each question, indicate in the space at the right the letter preceding the heading of the file drawer in which the record should be filed.

COLUMN I	COLUMN II			
11. Thomas Adams	A. Aab-Abi	I. Akp-Ald	11. ____
12. Joseph Albert	B. Abj-Ach	J. Ale-Amo	12. ____
13. Frank Anaster	C. Aci-Aco	K. Amp-Aor	13. ____
14. Charles Abt	D. Acp-Ada	L. Aos-Apr	14. ____
15. John Alfred	E. Adb-Afr	M. Aps-Asi	15. ____
16. Louis Aron	F. Afs-Ago	N. Asj-Ati	16. ____
17. Francis Amos	G. Agp-Ahz	O. Atj-Awz	17. ____
18. William Adler	H. Aia-Ako		18. ____

Questions: 19 - 28

DIRECTIONS: Questions 19 through 28 are to be answered on the basis of the usual rules of filing. Column I lists, next to the numbers 19 through 28, the names of 10 clinic patients. Column II lists, next to the letters A to D the headings of file drawers into which you are to place the medical records of these patients. For each question, indicate in the space at the right the letter preceding the heading of the file drawer in which the record should be filed.

COLUMN I		COLUMN II		
19.	Frank Shea	A.	Sab-Sej	19.___
20.	Rose Seaborn	B.	Sek-Sio	20.___
21.	Samuel Smollin	C.	Sip-Soo	21.___
22.	Thomas Shur	D.	Sop-Syz	22.___
23.	Ben Schaefer			23.___
24.	Shirley Strauss			24.___
25.	Harry Spiro			25.___
26.	Dora Skelly			26.___
27.	Sylvia Smith			27.___
28.	Arnold Selz			28.___

KEY (CORRECT ANSWERS)

1.	D	16.	M
2.	A	17.	J
3.	D	18.	E
4.	B	19.	B
5.	B	20.	A
6.	C	21.	C
7.	D	22.	B
8.	C	23.	A
9.	D	24.	D
10.	A	25.	D
11.	D	26.	C
12.	I	27.	C
13.	K	28.	B
14.	B		
15.	J		

ARITHMETICAL REASONING
EXAMINATION SECTION
TEST 1

DIRECTIONS: Each question or incomplete statement is followed by several suggested answers or completions. Select the one that BEST answers the question or completes the statement. *PRINT THE LETTER OF THE CORRECT ANSWER IN THE SPACE AT THE RIGHT.*

1. If a secretary answered 28 phone calls and typed the addresses for 112 credit statements in one morning, what is the RATIO of phone calls answered to credit statements typed for that period of time?

    A. 1:4   B. 1:7   C. 2:3   D. 3:5

1.____

2. According to a suggested filing system, no more than 10 folders should be filed behind any one file guide and from 15 to 25 file guides should be used in each file drawer for easy finding and filing.
The MAXIMUM number of folders that a five-drawer file cabinet can hold to allow easy finding and filing is

    A. 550   B. 750   C. 1,100   D. 1,250

2.____

3. An employee had a starting salary of $19,353. He received a salary increase at the end of each year, and at the end of the seventh year his salary was $25,107.
What was his AVERAGE annual increase in salary over these seven years?

    A. $765   B. $807   C. $822   D. $858

3.____

4. The 55 typists and 28 senior clerks in a certain agency were paid a total of $1,457,400 in salaries in 2005.
If the average annual salary of a typist was $16,800, the average annual salary of a senior clerk was

    A. $19,050   B. $19,950   C. $20,100   D. $20,250

4.____

5. A typist has been given a three-page report to type. She has finished typing the first two pages. The first page has 283 words, and the second page has 366 words.
If the total report consists of 954 words, how many words will she have to type on the third page of the report?

    A. 202   B. 287   C. 305   D. 313

5.____

6. In one day, Clerk A processed 30% more forms than Clerk B, and Clerk C processed 1 1/4 as many forms as Clerk A.
If Clerk B processed 40 forms, how many more forms were processed by Clerk C than Clerk B?

    A. 12   B. 13   C. 21   D. 25

6.____

7. A clerk who earns a gross salary of $678 every 2 weeks has the following deductions taken from her paycheck: 15% for city, state, and federal taxes; 2 1/2% for Social Security; $1.95 for health insurance; and $9.00 for union dues.
The amount of her take-home pay is

   A. $429.60   B. $468.60   C. $497.40   D. $548.40

7.____

8. In 2002, an agency spent $400 to buy pencils at a cost of $1.00 a dozen.
If the agency used 3/4 of these pencils in 2002 and used the same number of pencils in 2003, how many more pencils did it have to buy to have enough pencils for all of 2003?

   A. 1,200   B. 2,400   C. 3,600   D. 4,800

8.____

9. A clerk who worked in Agency X earned the following salaries: $15,105 the first year, $15,750 the second year, and $16,440 the third year. Another clerk who worked in Agency Y for three years earned $15,825 a year for two years and $16,086 the third year.
The DIFFERENCE between the average salaries received by both clerks over a three-year period is

   A. $147   B. $153   C. $261   D. $423

9.____

10. An employee who works more than 40 hours in any week receives overtime payment for the extra hours at time and one-half (1 1/2 times) his hourly rate of pay. An employee who earns $13.60 an hour works a total of 45 hours during a certain week.
His TOTAL pay for that week would be

   A. $564.40   B. $612.00   C. $646.00   D. $824.00

10.____

11. Suppose that the amount of money spent for supplies in 2006 for a division in a city department was $156,500. This represented an increase of 12% over the amount spent for supplies for this division in 2005.
The amount of money spent for supplies for this division in 2005 was MOST NEARLY

   A. $139,730   B. $137,720   C. $143,460   D. $138,720

11.____

12. Suppose that a group of five clerks have been assigned to insert 24,000 letters into envelopes. The clerks perform this work at the following rates of speed: Clerk A, 1,100 letters an hour; Clerk B, 1,450 letters an hour; Clerk C, 1,200 letters an hour; Clerk D, 1,300 letters an hour; Clerk E, 1,250 letters an hour. At the end of two hours of work, Clerks C and D are assigned to another task.
From the time that Clerks C and D were taken off the assignment, the number of hours required for the remaining clerks to complete this assignment is

   A. less than 3 hours
   B. 3 hours
   C. more than 3 hours, but less than 4 hours
   D. more than 4 hours

12.____

13. The number 60 is 40% of

   A. 24   B. 84   C. 96   D. 150

13.____

14. If 3/8 of a number is 96, the number is

   A. 132   B. 36   C. 256   D. 156

14.____

15. A city department uses an average of 25 20-cent, 35 30-cent, and 350 40-cent postage stamps each day.
    The TOTAL cost of stamps used by the department in a five-day period is   15.____

    A. $29.50   B. $155.50   C. $290.50   D. $777.50

16. A city department issued 12,000 applications in 2000. The number of applications that the department issued in 1998 was 25% greater than the number it issued in 2000. If the department issued 10% fewer applications in 1996 than it did in 1998, the number it issued in 1996 was   16.____

    A. 16,500   B. 13,500   C. 9,900   D. 8,100

17. A clerk can add 40 columns of figures an hour by using an adding machine and 20 columns of figures an hour without using an adding machine.
    The TOTAL number of hours it would take him to add 200 columns if he does 3/5 of the work by machine and the rest without the machine is   17.____

    A. 6   B. 7   C. 8   D. 9

18. In 1997, a city department bought 500 dozen pencils at $1.20 per dozen. In 2000, only 75 percent as many pencils were bought as were bought in 1997, but the price was 20 percent higher than the 1997 price. The TOTAL cost of the pencils bought in 2000 was   18.____

    A. $540   B. $562.50   C. $720   D. $750

19. A clerk is assigned to check the accuracy of the entries on 490 forms. He checks 40 forms an hour. After working one hour on this task, he is joined by another clerk, who checks these forms at the rate of 35 an hour.
    The TOTAL number of hours required to do the entire assignment is   19.____

    A. 5   B. 6   C. 7   D. 8

20. Assume that there are a total of 420 employees in a city agency. Thirty percent of the employees are clerks, and 1/7 are typists.
    The DIFFERENCE between the number of clerks and the number of typists is   20.____

    A. 126   B. 66   C. 186   D. 80

21. Assume that a duplicating machine produces copies of a bulletin at a cost of 2 cents per copy. The machine produces 120 copies of the bulletin per minute.
    If the cost of producing a certain number of copies was $12, how many minutes of operation did it take the machine to produce this number of copies?   21.____

    A. 5   B. 2   C. 10   D. 6

22. An assignment is completed by 32 clerks in 22 days. Assuming that all the clerks work at the same rate of speed, the number of clerks that would be needed to complete this assignment in 16 days is   22.____

    A. 27   B. 38   C. 44   D. 52

23. A department head hired a total of 60 temporary employees to handle a seasonal increase in the department's workload. The following lists the number of temporary employees hired, their rates of pay, and the duration of their employment:

    One-third of the total were hired as clerks, each at the rate of $27,500 a year, for two months.

    30 percent of the total were hired as office machine operators, each at the rate of $31,500 a year, for four months.

    22 stenographers were hired, each at the rate of $30,000 a year, for three months.

The total amount paid to these temporary employees was MOST NEARLY

    A. $1,780,000   B. $450,000
    C. $650,000   D. $390,000

23.____

24. Assume that there are 2,300 employees in a city agency. Also, assume that five percent of these employees are accountants, that 80 percent of the accountants have college degrees, and that one-half of the accountants who have college degrees have five years of experience. Then, the number of employees in the agency who are accountants with college degrees and five years of experience is

    A. 46   B. 51   C. 460   D. 920

24.____

25. Assume that the regular 8-hour working day of a laborer is from 8 A.M. to 5 P.M., with an hour off for lunch. He earns a regular hourly rate of pay for these 8 hours and is paid at the rate of time-and-a-half for each hour worked after his regular working day.
If, on a certain day, he works from 8 A.M. to 6 P.M., with an hour off for lunch, and earns $171, his regular hourly rate of pay is

    A. $16.30   B. $17.10   C. $18.00   D. $19.00

25.____

KEY (CORRECT ANSWERS)

1.	A		11.	A
2.	D		12.	B
3.	C		13.	D
4.	A		14.	C
5.	C		15.	D
6.	D		16.	B
7.	D		17.	B
8.	B		18.	A
9.	A		19.	C
10.	C		20.	B

21.	A
22.	C
23.	B
24.	A
25.	C

SOLUTIONS TO PROBLEMS

1. 28/112 is equivalent to 1:4

2. Maximum number of folders = (10)(25)(5) = 1250

3. Average annual increase = ($25,107-19,353) ÷ 7 = $822

4. $1,457,400 - (55)($16,800) = $533,400 = total amount paid to senior clerks. Average senior clerk's salary = $533,400 ÷ 28 = $19,050

5. Number of words on 3rd page = 954 - 283 - 366 = 305

6. Clerk A processed (40)(1.30) = 52 forms and clerk C processed (52)(1.25) = 65 forms. Finally, 65 - 40 = 25

7. Take-home pay = $678 - (.15)($678) - (.025)($678) - $1.95 - $9.00 = $548.40

8. (400)(12) = 4800 pencils. In 2002, (3/4)(4800) = 3600 were used, so that 1200 pencils were available at the beginning of 2003. Since 3600 pencils were also used in 2003, the agency had to buy 3600 - 1200 = 2400 pencils.

9. Average salary for clerk in Agency X = ($15,105+$15,750+$16,440)/3 = $15,765. Average salary for clerk in Agency Y = ($15,825+ $15,825+$16,086) ÷ 3 = $15,912. Difference in average salaries = $147.

10. Total pay = ($13.60)(40) + ($20.40)(5) = $646.00

11. In 2005, amount spent = $156,500 ÷ 1.12 ≈ $139,730 (Actual value = $139,732.1429)

12. At the end of 2 hours, (1100)(2) + (1450)(2) + (1200)(2) + (1300X2) + (1250X2) = 12,600 letters have been inserted into envelopes. The remaining 11,400 letters done by clerks A, B, and C will require 11,400 ÷ (1100+1450+1250) = 3 hours.

13. 60 ÷ .40 = 150

14. 96 ÷ 3/8 = (96)(8/3) = 256

15. Total cost = (5)[(25)(.20)+(35)(.30)+(350)(.40)]= $777.50

16. In 1998, (12,000) (1.25) = 15,000 applications were issued In 1996, (15,000)(.90) = 13,500 applications were issued

17. Total number of hours $=\dfrac{120}{40} + \dfrac{80}{20} = 7$

18. (.75)(500 dozen) = 375 dozen purchased in 2000 at a cost of ($1.20)(1.20) = $1.44 per dozen. Total cost for 2000 = ($1.44) (375) = $540

19. Total time = 1 hour + 450/75 hrs. = 7 hours

20. (.30)(420) - (1/7)(420) = 126 - 60 = 66

21. Cost per minute = (120)(.02) = $2.40. Then, $12 ÷ $2.40 = 5 minutes

22. (32)(22) ÷ 16 = 44 clerks

23. Total amount paid = (20)($27,500)(2/12) + (18)($31,500) (4/12) + (22)($30,000)(3/12) = $445,666.$\overline{6}$ ≈ $450,000

24. Number of accountants with college degrees and five years of experience = (2300)(.05)(.80)(1/2) = 46

25. Let x = regular hourly pay. Then, (8)(x) + (1)(1.5x) = $1.71 So, 9.5x = 171. Solving, x = $18

———

TEST 2

DIRECTIONS: Each question or incomplete statement is followed by several suggested answers or completions. Select the one that BEST answers the question or completes the statement. *PRINT THE LETTER OF THE CORRECT ANSWER IN THE SPACE AT THE RIGHT.*

1. Assume that you know the capacity of a filing cabinet, the extent of which it is filled, and the daily rate at which material is being added to the file.
   In order to estimate how many more days it will take for the cabinet to be filled to capacity, you should

   A. divide the extent to which the cabinet is filled by the daily rate
   B. take the difference between the capacity of the cabinet and the material in it, and multiply the result by the daily rate of adding material
   C. divide the daily rate of adding material by the difference between the capacity of the cabinet and the material in it
   D. take the difference between the capacity of the cabinet and the material in it, and divide the result by the daily rate of adding material

1.____

2. Suppose you have been asked to compute the average salary earned in your department during the past year. For each of the divisions of the department, you are given the number of employees and the average salary.
   In order to find the requested overall average salary for the department, you should

   A. add the average salaries of the various divisions and divide the total by the number of divisions
   B. multiply the number of employees in each division by the corresponding average salary, add the results and divide the total by the number of employees in the department
   C. add the average salaries of the various divisions and divide the total by the total number of employees in the department
   D. multiply the sum of the average salaries of the various divisions by the total number of divisions and divide the resulting product by the total number of employees in the department

2.____

3. Suppose that a group of six clerks has been assigned to assemble the duplicated pages of a report into completed copies. After four hours of work, they have been able to complete one-third of the job.
   In order to assemble all the remaining copies in three more hours of work, the number of clerks which will have to be added to the original six, assuming that all the clerks assigned to this task work at the same rate of speed, is

   A. 10   B. 16   C. 2   D. 6

3.____

4. A study of the grades of students in a certain college revealed that in 2005, 15% fewer students received a passing grade in mathematics than in 2004, whereas in 2006 the number of students passing mathematics increased 15% over 2005.
   On the basis of this study, it would be MOST accurate to conclude that

   A. the same percentage of students passed mathematics in 2004 as in 2006
   B. of the three years studied, the greatest percentage of students passed mathematics in 2006

4.____

C.   the percentage of students who passed mathematics in 2006 was less than the percentage passing this subject in 2004

D.   the percentage of students passing mathematics in 2004 was 15% greater than the percentage of students passing this subject in 2006

5.   A city department employs 1,400 people, of whom 35% are clerks and 1/8 are stenographers.
The number of employees in the department who are neither clerks nor stenographers is

   A.   640   B.   665   C.   735   D.   760

5.___

6.   Assume that there are 190 papers to be filed and that Clerk A and Clerk B are assigned to file these papers. If Clerk A files 40 papers more than Clerk B, then the number of papers that Clerk A files is

   A.   75   B.   110   C.   115   D.   150

6.___

7.   A stock clerk had on hand the following items:
       500 pads, each worth 16 cents
       130 pencils, each worth 12 cents
       50 dozen rubber bands, worth 8 cents a dozen
If, from this stock, he issued 125 pads, 45 pencils, and 48 rubber bands, the value of the remaining stock would be

   A. $25.72   B. $27.80   C. $70.52   D. $73.88

7.___

8.   In a particular agency, there were 160 accidents in 2002. Of these accidents, 75% were due to unsafe acts and the rest were due to unsafe conditions. In the following year, a special safety program was established. The number of accidents in 2004 due to unsafe acts was reduced to 35% of what it had been in 2002.
How many accidents due to unsafe acts were there in 2004?

   A.   20   B.   36   C.   42   D.   56

8.___

9.   At the end of every month, the petty cash fund of Agency A is reimbursed for payments made from the fund during the month. During the month of February, the amounts paid from the fund were entered on receipts as follows: 10 bus fares of $1.40 each and one taxi fare of $14.00. At the end of the month, the money left in the fund was in the following denominations: 60 one-dollar bills, 16 quarters, 40 dimes, and 80 nickels.
If the petty cash fund is reduced by 20% for the following month, how much money will there be available in the petty cash fund for March?

   A. $44   B. $80   C. $86   D. $100

9.___

10.   An employee worked on a job for 6 weeks, 5 days per week, and 8 hours per day.
How many hours did he work on the job?

   A.   40   B.   48   C.   55   D.   240

10.___

11.   Divide 35 by .7.

   A.   5   B.   42   C.   50   D.   245

11.___

12. .1% of 25 =   12.____

    A. .025   B. .25   C. 2.5   D. 25

13. In a city agency, 80 percent of the total number of employees are more than 25 years of age and 65 percent of the total number of employees are high school graduates. The SMALLEST possible percent of employees who are both high school graduates and more than 25 years of age is   13.____

    A. 35%   B. 45%   C. 55%   D. 65%

14. Two clerical units, X and Y, each having a different number of clerks, are assigned to file registration cards. It takes Unit X, which contains 8 clerks, 21 days to file the same number of cards that Unit Y can file in 28 days. It is also a fact that Unit X can file 174,528 cards in 72 days.
Assuming that all the clerks in both units work at the same rate of speed, the number of cards which can be filed by Unit Y in 144 days, if 4 more clerks are added to the staff of Unit Y, is MOST NEARLY   14.____

    A. 392,000   B. 436,000   C. 523,000   D. 669,000

15. Assume that two machines, each costing $14,750, were purchased for your office. Each machine requires the services of an operator at a salary of $2,000 per month. These machines are to replace six clerks, two of whom earn $1,550 per month each, and four of whom earn $1,700 per month each.
The number of months it will take for the cost of the machines to be made up from the savings in salaries is   15.____

    A. less than four   B. four
    C. five   D. more than five

16. Suppose that the amount of stationery used by your department in August decreased by 16% as compared with the amount used in July, and that the amount used in September increased by 25% as compared with the amount used in August.
The amount of stationery used in September as compared with the amount used in July is   16.____

    A. greater by 5 percent   B. less by 5 percent
    C. greater by 9 percent   D. the same

17. An employee earns $48 a day and works 5 days a week.
He will earn $2,160 in _____ weeks.   17.____

    A. 5   B. 7   C. 8   D. 9

18. In a certain bureau, the entire staff consists of 1 senior supervisor, 2 supervisors, 6 assistant supervisors, and 54 associate workers.
The percent of the staff who are not associate workers is MOST NEARLY   18.____

    A. 14   B. 21   C. 27   D. 32

19. In a certain bureau, five employees each earn $1,000 a month, another 3 employees each earn $2,200 a month, and another two employees each earn $1,400 a month.
The monthly payroll for these employees is   19.____

    A. $3,600   B. $8,800   C. $11,400   D. $14,400

20. An employee contributes 5% of his salary to the pension fund.
If his salary is $1,200 a month, the amount of his contribution to the pension fund in a year is

    A. $480　　　B. $720　　　C. $960　　　D. $1,200　　　20.____

21. The number of square feet in an area that is 50 feet long and 30 feet wide is

    A. 80　　　B. 150　　　C. 800　　　D. 1,500　　　21.____

22. A farm hand was paid a weekly wage of $332.16 for a 48-hour work week. As a result of a new labor contract, he is paid $344.96 a week for a 44-hour work week with time and one-half pay for time worked in excess of 44 hours in any work week.
If he continues to work 48 hours weekly under the new contract, the amount by which his average hourly rate for a 48-hour work week under the new contract exceeds the hourly rate previously paid him lies between _____ and _____ cents, inclusive.　　　22.____

    A. 91;100　　　B. 101;110　　　C. 111;120　　　D. 121;130

23. Each side of a square room, which is being used as an office, measures 66 feet. The floor of the room is divided by six traffic aisles, each aisle being six feet wide. Three of the aisles run parallel to the east and west sides of the room, and the other three run parallel to the north and south sides of the room, so that the remaining floor space is divided into 16 equal sections. If all of the floor space which is not being used for traffic aisles is occupied by desk and chair sets, and each set takes up 24 square feet of floor space, the number of desk and chair sets in the room is　　　23.____

    A. 80　　　B. 64　　　C. 36　　　D. 96

24. In 2005, a city agency bought 12,000 envelopes at $4.00 per hundred. In 2006, the price of envelopes purchased was 40 percent higher than the 2005 price, but only 60 percent as many envelopes were bought.
The total cost of the envelopes purchased in 2006 was MOST NEARLY　　　24.____

    A. $250　　　B. $320　　　C. $400　　　D. $480

25. In a city agency, 25 percent of the women employees and 50 percent of the men employees attended a general staff meeting.
If 48 percent of all the employees in the agency are women, the percentage of all the employees who attended the meeting is　　　25.____

    A. 36%　　　B. 37%　　　C. 38%　　　D. 75%

KEY (CORRECT ANSWERS)

1. D	11. C
2. B	12. A
3. A	13. B
4. C	14. A
5. C	15. C
6. C	16. A
7. D	17. D
8. C	18. A
9. B	19. D
10. D	20. B

21. D
22. D
23. D
24. C
25. C

SOLUTIONS TO PROBLEMS

1. To determine number of days required to fill cabinet to capacity, subtract material in it from capacity amount, then divide by daily rate of adding material. Example: A cabinet already has 10 folders in it, and the capacity is 100 folders. Suppose 5 folders per day are added. Number of days to fill to capacity = $(100-10) \div 5 = 18$

2. To determine overall average salary, multiply number of employees in each division by that division's average salary, add results, then divide by total number of employees. Example: Division A has 4 employees with average salary of \$40,000; division B has 6 employees with average salary of \$36,000; division C has 2 employees with average salary of \$46,000. Average salary = $[(4)(\$40,000)+(6)(\$36,000)+(2)(\$46,000)] / 12 = \$39,000$

3. $(6)(4) = 24$ clerk-hours. Since only one-third of work has been done, $(24)(3) - 24 = 48$ clerk-hours remain. Then, $48 \div 3 = 16$ clerks. Thus, $16 - 6 = 10$ additional clerks.

4. The percentage of students passing math in 2006 was less than the percentage of those passing math in 2004. Example: Suppose 400 students passed math in 2004. Then, $(400)(.85) = 340$ passed in 2005. Finally, $(340)(1.15) = 391$ passed in 2006.

5. $1400 - (.35)(1400) - (1/8)(1400) = 735$

6. Let x = number of papers filed by clerk A, x-40 = number of papers filed by clerk B. Then, $x + (x-40) = 190$ Solving, $x = 115$

7. $(500-125)(.16) + (130-45)(.12) + (50 - 48/12)(.08) = \$60.00 + \$10.20 + \$3.68 = \$73.88$

8. $(160)(.75) = 120$ accidents due to unsafe acts in 2002. In 2004, $(120)(.35) = 42$ accidents due to unsafe acts

9. Original amount at beginning of February in the fund = $(10)(\$1.40) + (1)(\$14.00) + (60)(\$1) + (16)(.25) + (40)(.10) + (80)(.05) = \$100$. Finally, for March, $(\$100)(.80) = \$80$ will be available

10. Total hours = $(6)(5)(8) = 240$

11. $35 \div .7 = 50$

12. .1% of 25 = $(.001)(25) = .025$

13. Let A = percent of employees who are at least 25 years old and B = percent of employees who are high school graduates. Also, let N = percent of employees who fit neither category and J = percent of employees who are in both categories.
    Then, $100 = A + B + N - J$. Substituting, $100 = 80 + 65 + N - J$ To minimize J, let N = 0. So, $100 = 80 + 65 + 0 - J$. Solving, $J = 45$

14. Let Y = number of clerks in Unit Y. Then, $(8)(21) = (4)(28)$, so Y = 6. Unit X has 8 clerks who can file 174,528 cards in 72 flays; thus, each clerk in Unit X can file $174,528 \div 72 \div 8 = 303$ cards per day. Adding 4 clerks to Unit Y will yield 10 clerks in that unit. Since their rate is equal to that of Unit X, the clerks in Unit Y will file, in 144 days, is $(303)(10)(144) = 436,320 \approx 436,000$ cards.

15. Let x = required number of months. The cost of the machines in x months = (2)(14,750) + (2)(2000)(x) = 29,500 + 4000x. The savings in salaries for the displaced clerks = x[(2)(1550) +(4)(1700)] = 9900x. Thus, 29,500 + 4000x = 9900x. Solving, x = 5. So, five months will elapse in order to achieve a savings in cost.

16. Let x = amount used in July, so that .84x = amount used in August. For September, the amount used = (.84x)(1.25) = 1.05x. This means the amount used in September is 5% more than the amount used in July.

17. Each week he earns ($48)(5) = $240. Then, $2160 ÷ $240 = 9 weeks

18. (1+2+6) ÷ 63 = 1/7 ≈ 14%

19. Monthly payroll = (5)($1000) + (3)($2200) + (2)($1400) = $14,400

20. Yearly contribution to pension fund = (12)($1200)(.05) = $720

21. (50')(30') = 1500 sq.ft.

22. Old rate = 332.16 ÷ 48 = 6.92 (48 hours)
    New rate = 344.96 (44 hours)
    Overtime rate = 344.96 ÷ 44 = 7.75/hr. x 1.5 x 4 = 46.48
    344.96 + 46.48 = 391.44
    391.44 ÷ 48 = 8.15
    815 - 692 = 123 cents an hour more

23. Each of the 16 sections is a square with side [66'-(3)(6')] ÷ 4 = 12'. So each section contains (12')(12') = 144 sq.ft.
    The number of desk and chair sets = (144 ÷ 24) (16) = 96

24. In 2006, (.60)(12,000) = 7200 envelopes were bought and the price per hundred was ($4.00)(1.40) = $5.60. The total cost = (5.60)(72) = $403.20 ≈ $400

25. (.25)(.48) + (.50)(.52) = .38 = 38%

TEST 3

DIRECTIONS: Each question or incomplete statement is followed by several suggested answers or completions. Select the one that BEST answers the question or completes the statement. *PRINT THE LETTER OF THE CORRECT ANSWER IN THE SPACE AT THE RIGHT.*

1. According to one suggested filing system, no more than 12 folders should be filed behind any one file guide and from 10 to 20 file guides should be used in each file drawer. Based on this filing system, the MAXIMUM number of folders that a four-drawer file cabinet can hold is

    1.___

    A. 240   B. 480   C. 960   D. 1,200

2. A certain office uses three different forms. Last year, it used 3,500 copies of Form L, 6,700 copies of Form M, and 10,500 copies of Form P. This year, the office expects to decrease the use of each of these forms by 5%. The TOTAL number of these three forms which the office expects to use this year is

    2.___

    A. 10,350   B. 16,560   C. 19,665   D. 21,735

3. The hourly rate of pay for a certain part-time employee is computed by dividing his yearly salary rate by the number of hours in the work year. The employee's yearly salary rate is $18,928, and there are 1,820 hours in the work year.
    If this employee works 18 hours during one week, his TOTAL earnings for these 18 hours are

    3.___

    A. $180.00   B. $183.60   C. $187.20   D. $190.80

4. Assume that the regular work week of an employee is 35 hours and that the employee is paid for any extra hours worked according to the following schedule. For hours worked in excess of 35 hours, up to and including 40 hours, the employee receives his regular hourly rate of pay. For hours worked in excess of 40 hours, the employee receives 1 1/2 times his hourly rate of pay.
    If the employee's hourly rate of pay is $11.20 and he works 43 hours during a certain week, his TOTAL pay for the week would be

    4.___

    A. $481.60   B. $498.40   C. $556.00   D. $722.40

5. A clerk divided his 35 hour work week as follows:
    1/5 of his time in sorting mail;
    1/2 of his time in filing letters; and
    1/7 of his time in reception work.
    The rest of his time was devoted to messenger work. The percentage of time spent on messenger work by the clerk during the week was MOST NEARLY

    5.___

    A. 6%   B. 10%   C. 14%   D. 16%

6. A city department has set up a computing unit and has rented 5 computing machines at a yearly rental of $700 per machine. In addition, the cost to the department for the maintenance and repair of each of these machines is $50 per year. Five computing machine operators, each receiving an annual salary of $15,000, and a supervisor, who receives $19,000 a year, have been assigned to this unit. This unit will perform the work previously performed by 10 employees whose combined salary was $162,000 a year.
    On the basis of these facts, the savings that will result from the operation of this computing unit for 5 years will be MOST NEARLY

    6.___

    A. $250,000   B. $320,000   C. $330,000   D. $475,000

7. Twelve clerks are assigned to enter certain data on index cards. This number of clerks could perform the task in 18 days. After these clerks have worked on this assignment for 6 days, 4 more clerks are added to the staff to do this work.
Assuming that all the clerks work at the same rate of speed, the entire task, instead of taking 18 days, will be performed in _____ days.

    A. 9   B. 12   C. 15   D. 16

7.____

8. Suppose that a file cabinet, which has a capacity of 3,000 cards, now contains approximately 2,200 cards. Cards are added to the file at the average rate of 30 cards a day.
To find the number of days it will take to fill the cabinet to capacity,

    A.   divide 3,000 by 30
    B.   divide 2,200 by 3,000
    C.   divide 800 by 30
    D.   multiply 30 by the fraction 2,200 divided by 3,000

8.____

9. Six gross of special drawing pencils were purchased for use in a city department.
If the pencils were used at the rate of 24 a week, the MAXIMUM number of weeks that the six gross of pencils would last is _____ weeks.

    A. 6   B. 12   C. 24   D. 36

9.____

10. A stock clerk had 600 pads on hand. He then issued 3/8 of his supply of pads to Division X, 1/4 to Division Y, and 1/6 to Division Z.
The number of pads remaining in stock is

    A. 48   B. 125   C. 240   D. 475

10.____

11. If a certain job can be performed by 18 clerks in 26 days, the number of clerks needed to perform the job in 12 days is _____ clerks.

    A. 24   B. 30   C. 39   D. 52

11.____

12. In anticipation of a seasonal increase in the amount of work to be performed by his division, a division chief prepared the following list of additional temporary employees needed by his division and the amount of time they would be employed:
    26 cashiers, each at $24,000 a year, for 2 months
    15 laborers, each at $85.00 a day, for 50 days
    6 clerks, each at $21,000 a year, for 3 months
The total approximate cost for this additional personnel would be MOST NEARLY

    A. $200,000   B. $250,000   C. $500,000   D. $600,000

12.____

13. A copy machine company offered to sell a city agency 4 copy machines at a discount of 15% from the list price, and to allow the agency $850 for each of its two old machines.
The list price of the new machines is $6,250 per machine.
If the city agency accepts this offer, the amount of money it will have to provide for the purchase of these 4 machines is

    A. $17,350   B. $22,950   C. $19,550   D. $18,360

13.____

14. A stationery buyer was offered bond paper at the following price scale: 14.___
      $1.43 per ream for the first 1,000 reams
      $1.30 per ream for the next 4,000 reams
      $1.20 per ream for each additional ream beyond 5,000 reams
    If the buyer ordered 10,000 reams of paper, the average cost per ream, computed to
    the nearest cent, was

      A. $1.24   B. $1.26   C. $1.31   D. $1.36

15. A clerk has 5.70 percent of his salary deducted for his retirement pension.   15.___
    If this clerk's annual salary is $20,400, the monthly deduction for his retirement pen-
    sion is

      A. $298.20   B. $357.90   C. $1,162.80   D. $96.90

16. In a certain bureau, two-thirds of the employees are clerks and the remainder are typists.   16.___
    If there are 90 clerks, then the number of typists in this bureau is

      A. 135   B. 45   C. 120   D. 30

17. The number of investigations conducted by an agency in 1999 was 3,600. In 2000, the   17.___
    number of investigations conducted was one-third more than in 1999. The number of
    investigations conducted in 2001 was three-fourths of the number conducted in 2000. It
    is anticipated that the number of investigations conducted in 2002 will be equal to the
    average of the three preceding years. On the basis of this information, the MOST accu-
    rate of the following statements is that the number of investigations conducted in

      A.   1999 is larger than the number anticipated for 2002
      B.   2000 is smaller than the number anticipated for 2002
      C.   2001 is equal to the number conducted in 1999
      D.   2001 is larger than the number anticipated in 2002

18. A city agency engaged in repair work uses a small part which the city purchases for 14   18.___
    each. Assume that, in a certain year, the total expenditure of the city for this part was
    $700.
    How many of these parts were purchased that year?

      A. 50   B. 200   C. 2,000   D. 5,000

19. The work unit which you supervise is responsible for processing 15 reports per month.   19.___
    If your unit has 4 clerks and the best worker completes 40% of the reports himself, how
    many reports would each of the other clerks have to complete if they all do an equal
    number?

      A. 1   B. 2   C. 3   D. 4

20. Assume that the work unit in which you work has 24 clerks and 18 stenographers. 20.____
   In order to change the ratio of stenographers to clerks so that there is 1 stenographer
   for every 4 clerks, it would be necessary to REDUCE the number of stenographers by

   A. 3   B. 6   C. 9   D. 12

21. The arithmetic mean salary for five employees earning $18,500, $18,300, $18,600, 21.____
   $18,400, and $18,500, respectively, is

   A. $18,450   B. $18,460   C. $18,475   D. $18,500

22. Last year, a city department which is responsible for purchasing supplies ordered bond 22.____
   paper in equal quantities from 22 different companies. The price was exactly the same
   for each company, and the total cost for the 22 orders was $693,113.
   Assuming prices did not change during the year, the cost of each order was MOST
   NEARLY

   A. $31,490   B. $31,495   C. $31,500   D. $31,505

23. Suppose that a large bureau has 187 employees. On a particular day, approximately 23.____
   14% of these employees are not available for work because of absences due to vacation,
   illness, or other reasons. Of the remaining employees, 1/7 are assigned to a special
   project while the balance are assigned to the normal work of the bureau. The number of
   employees assigned to the normal work of the bureau on that day is

   A. 112   B. 124   C. 138   D. 142

24. Suppose that you are in charge of a typing pool of 8 typists. Two typists type at the rate of 24.____
   38 words per minute; three type at the rate of 40 words per minute; three type at the rate
   of 42 words per minute. The average typewritten page consists of 50 lines, 12 words per
   line. Each employee works from 9 to 5 with one hour off for lunch.
   The total number of pages typed by this pool in one day is, on the average, CLOSEST
   to _____ pages.

   A. 205   B. 225   C. 250   D. 275

25. Suppose that part-time workers are paid $7.20 an hour, prorated to the nearest half hour, 25.____
   with pay guaranteed for a minimum of four hours if services are required for less than
   four hours. In one operation, part-time workers signed the time sheet as follows:

Worker	In		Out	
A	8:00	A.M.	11:35	A.M.
B	8:30	A.M.	3:20	P.M.
C	7:55	A.M.	11:00	A.M.
D	8:30	A.M.	2:25	P.M.

   How much would TOTAL payment to these part-time workers amount to for this operation, assuming that those who stayed after 12 Noon were not paid for one hour which
   they took off for lunch?

   A. $134.40   B. $136.80   C. $142.20   D. $148.80

147

KEY (CORRECT ANSWERS)

1.	C	11.	C
2.	C	12.	A
3.	C	13.	C
4.	B	14.	B
5.	D	15.	D
6.	B	16.	B
7.	C	17.	C
8.	C	18.	D
9.	D	19.	C
10.	B	20.	D

21.	B
22.	D
23.	C
24.	B
25.	B

SOLUTIONS TO PROBLEMS

1. Maximum number of folders = (4)(12)(20) = 960

2. (3500+6700+10,500)(.95) = 19,665

3. Hourly rate = $18,928 ÷ 1820 = $10.40. Then, the pay for 18 hours = ($10.40)(18) = $187.20

4. Total pay = ($11.20)(40) + ($11.20)(1.5)(3) = $498.40

5. (1 - 1/5 - 1/2 - 1/7)(100)% ≈ 16%

6. Previous cost for five years = ($324,000)(5) = $1,620,000
   Present cost for five years = (5)(5)($1,400) + (5)(5)($100) + (5)(5)($30,000) + (1)(5)($38,000) = $977,500   The net savings = $642,500 ≈ $640,000

7. (12)(18) = 216 clerk-days. Then, 216 - (12)(6) = 144 clerk-days of work left when 4 more clerks are added. Now, 16 clerks will finish the task in 144 ÷ 16 = 9 more days. Finally, the task will require a total of 6 + 9 = 15 days.

8. Number of days needed = (3000-2200) ÷ 30 = 26.7, which is equivalent to dividing 800 by 30.

9. (6)(144) = 864 pencils purchased. Then, 864 ÷ 24 = 36 maximum number of weeks

10. Number of remaining pads = 600 - (1)(600) - (1/4)(600) - (1/6)(600) = 125

11. (18)(26) ÷ 12 = 39 clerks

12. Total cost = (26)($24,000)(2/12) + (15)($85)(50) + (6)($21,000)(3/12) = $199,250 $200,000

13. (4)($6250)(.85) - (2)($850) = $19,550

14. Total cost = ($1.43)(1000) + ($1.30)(4000) + ($1.20X5000) = $12,630. Average cost per ream = $12,630 10,000 ≈ $1.26

15. Monthly salary = $20,400 ÷ 12 = $1700. Thus, the monthly deduction for his pension = ($1700)(.057) + $96.90

16. Number of employees = 90 ÷ 2/3 = 135. Then, the number of typists = (1/3)(135) = 45

17. The number of investigations for each year is as follows:
    1999: 3600
    2000: (3600)(1 1/3) = 4800
    2001: (4800)(3/4) = 3600
    2002: (3600+4800+3600)/3 = 4000
    So, the number of investigations were equal for 1999 and 2001.

18. $700 ÷ .14 = 5000 parts

19. The best worker does (.40)(15) = 6 reports. The other 9 reports are divided equally among the other 3 clerks, so each clerk does 9 ÷ 3 = 3 reports.

20. 1:4 = 6:24 . Thus, the number of stenographers must be reduced by 18 - 6 = 12

21. Mean = ($18,500+$18,300+$18,400+$18,500) ÷ 5 = $18,460

22. The cost per order = $693,113 ÷ 22 ≈ $31,505

23. 187 - (.14) = 26. 187 - 26 = 161 - 1/7 (161) = 23
    161 - 23 = 138

24. Number of words typed in 1 min. = (2)(38) + (3)(40) + (3)(42) = 322. For 7 hours, the total number of words typed = (7)(60)(322) = 135,240. Each page contains (on the average) (50)(12) = 600 words. Finally, 135,240 ÷ 600 ≈ 225 pages

25. Worker A = ($7.20)(4) = $28.80
    Worker B = ($7.20)(3 1/2) + ($7.20)(2 1/2) = $43.20
    Worker C = ($7.20)(4) = $28.80
    Worker D = ($7.20)(3 1/2) + ($7.20)(1 1/2) = $36.00
    Total for all 4 workers = $136.80
    Note: Workers A and C received the guaranteed minimum 4 hours pay each.